The Art of THE HOBBIT
by J.R.R. Tolkien

Also by Wayne G. Hammond & Christina Scull

J.R.R. Tolkien: Artist & Illustrator
Letters of J.R.R. Tolkien (*Index*)
The Lord of the Rings: A Reader's Companion
The J.R.R. Tolkien Companion & Guide

As editors of works by J.R.R. Tolkien

Roverandom
Farmer Giles of Ham (50th anniversary edition)
The Lord of the Rings (50th anniversary edition)

The Art of
THE HOBBIT
by J.R.R. Tolkien

Wayne G. Hammond *&* Christina Scull

HarperCollins*Publishers*

HarperCollins*Publishers*
77–85 Fulham Palace Road
Hammersmith, London w6 8jb
www.tolkien.co.uk

www.tolkienestate.com

Published by HarperCollins*Publishers* 2011

3 5 7 9 8 6 4

A catalogue record for this book is available from the British Library

ISBN 978-0-00-744081-8

Set in Adobe Minion Pro

Printed and bound in China

TITLE-PAGE Detail from *Thror's Map* (fig. 28)
OPPOSITE Detail from final dust-jacket art for *The Hobbit* (fig. 101)

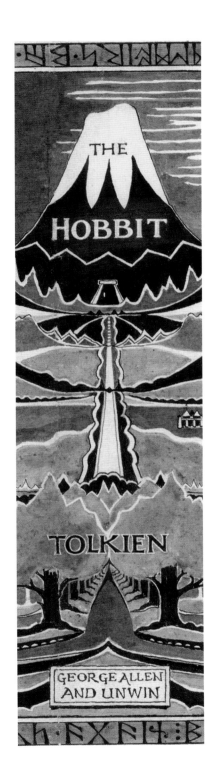

Contents

The hill : hobbiton-across-the Water

The Hobbit

or

There and Back
Again

by

J. R. R. Tolkien

Illustrated
by the Author

London
George Allen & Unwin Ltd
Museum Street

The Hobbit, title-spread for the second printing (1937)

Introduction

This book, with the help of maps, does not need any illustrations it is good and should appeal to all children between the ages of 5 and 9.

The book in question was *The Hobbit*, and the judgement was by Rayner Unwin, the ten-year-old son of Stanley Unwin, who was considering Tolkien's story for publication. In 1936, at his father's request, Rayner read *The Hobbit* in typescript and returned an enthusiastic report. For this he was paid a shilling – the best shilling George Allen & Unwin ever spent, Rayner would later say, since it led to the publication of one of the firm's most successful books, and in turn to an enormously popular sequel, *The Lord of the Rings*.

Rayner's comment that *The Hobbit* should include maps may have been suggested by the presence with the typescript of one of those Tolkien had drawn to accompany his story; or it may already have been agreed between Tolkien and Allen & Unwin that maps would be needed, as aids to the reader, should *The Hobbit* be published. But Rayner's view that the work did not need illustrations – a nod, maybe, to the publisher's perennial desire to control costs – ultimately was not shared by its author. For even though *The Hobbit* had been submitted originally with only one image (probably a version of *Thror's Map*, which is mentioned in the text), it was a more fully illustrated book as it was read by (or to) family and friends, and Tolkien wished it to remain so when it was presented to a wider audience.

By the time he sent *The Hobbit* to Allen & Unwin, J.R.R. Tolkien had been an amateur artist for more than thirty years. Born in 1892, he belonged to an age when painting and drawing were still common recreations, cheap entertainment for children as well as acceptable social pursuits by ladies and gentlemen. He was self-taught, except for whatever instruction he received from his mother (who died when he was only twelve) or whatever techniques he may have learned from other relations, such as his maternal grandfather, John Suffield, who drew his own Christmas cards and wrote a beautiful script. Early inspiration for Tolkien's art came from places he knew as a boy and young man – the Cobb at Lyme Regis, fields and houses of Berkshire, rocks and sea on the Cornwall coast, delphiniums and foxgloves in the garden of his cousins in Worcestershire. He took particular delight in landscapes and in architecture; there are comparatively few figures or portraits in his work, and his talent to produce them was limited. His greatest skill was in rendering flowers, trees, and other features of the natural world.

From at least 1911, soon after he became an undergraduate at Oxford, Tolkien began to draw as well from the imagination. He made a series of pictures of symbolic or abstract visions, such as *Before* and *Afterwards*, *Undertenishness* and *Grownupishness*. (A selection is reproduced in our book *J.R.R. Tolkien: Artist and Illustrator*.) Some of these are exceedingly strange – one can only guess what Tolkien had in mind. Others are clearly related to works of literature: *Xanadu*, after the poem 'Kubla Khan' by Samuel Taylor Coleridge, and *The Land of Pohja* from the Finnish *Kalevala*. But most notable are a handful of images which illustrate, or themselves inspired, writings by Tolkien himself; for by this stage, during the first years of the First World War, he had begun to create a private mythology or body of legends which came to be known as 'The Silmarillion'.

The seed of his mythology, Tolkien said, was his desire to invent languages, and the realization that invented languages must exist in the context of invented places and peoples. But he was also driven by a passion to tell stories, at first through poetry and later also in prose. His tales of Beren and Lúthien, of the fall of the Elvish realms of Gondolin and Nargothrond, of Eärendil the mariner, of Fëanor and the great jewels known as the Silmarils, and so many more concerning Elves, Dwarves, and Men, developed over decades. They were his life's work, left at his death (in 1973) to be edited for publication by his son Christopher, beginning with *The Silmarillion* in 1977. His words are dramatic and full of memorable images; but some of the 'Silmarillion' stories also found vivid expression in his drawings and water-colours, in particular during an exceptionally productive span in the late 1920s. Among the splendid pictures he made at that time was a view of the dense forest of Taur-nu-Fuin, later redrawn as *Mirkwood* for the first printings of *The Hobbit*.

The 1920s in general were an important period for Tolkien. From 1920 to 1925 he taught on the English faculty of the University of Leeds, and in 1925 took up the first of two professorial chairs in the Oxford English School. He had become a father in 1917, with the birth of his son John, and by the end of the next decade, he and his wife Edith had three more children: Michael in 1920, Christopher in 1924, and Priscilla in 1929. They were an eager audience for stories, and Tolkien was glad to oblige.

Some of these stories arrived in the form of letters, which he wrote to his children almost every December from 1920 through 1943 as if from Father Christmas and his friends, telling of adventures or mishaps at the North Pole. Each letter was made to appear 'genuine' by the use of distinctive scripts – Father Christmas, for instance, who was nearly two thousand years old, had a very shaky hand – and with faux North Pole stamps and postmarks. Most of the letters included at least one illustration, often strikingly decorative. Of no less quality were some of the illustrations Tolkien made for *Roverandom*, the story of a dog magically turned into a toy, which he first told in 1925. The earliest written version of his *Farmer Giles of Ham* probably also was set down in the second half of the 1920s, but for that story Tolkien for some reason drew no pictures. Finally, around the end of the decade or perhaps early in the 1930s, he produced a picture book, combining words and art in equal measure, concerned with an impulsive, eccentric character called Mr Bliss and his misadventures with a motor-car.

Tolkien was inspired by his children to invent tales which appealed to young listeners, in a contemporary if often paternal voice, and in a relatively short form. At the same time, the 'Silmarillion' legends continued to occupy his thoughts: an epic narrative set across aeons of tragic history, told in a 'high' style and with sometimes archaic language. Then, around 1930 (the evidence is too contradictory to give a precise date), he began to write a work which blended these two varieties of storytelling, and to a degree borrowed from the mythology – a work for children (John, Michael, and Christopher were its primary audience; Priscilla was still too young), but with qualities of depth and vision its critics, once it was published, found hard to define. The anonymous reviewer in the *Times Literary Supplement* of 2 October 1937 – in fact

Tolkien's great friend C.S. Lewis, who had inside knowledge – came closest in saying that *The Hobbit* admitted its readers to 'a world that seems to have been going on before we stumbled into it'.

Tolkien recalled jotting the now famous first line of *The Hobbit* ('In a hole in the ground there lived a hobbit') idly in a school examination booklet. That sheet has been lost, along with most of the earliest known manuscript of the work: only six pages survive, one of which includes a sketch of *Thror's Map*. This fragment was followed by a typescript and manuscripts, in the course of which Tolkien drew further maps, of the areas between the Misty Mountains and Mirkwood and surrounding the Lonely Mountain. He seems to have devised the story of *The Hobbit* in stages. It was a feature of his sons' winter 'reads' after evening tea (that is, it was read to them by their father), as Christopher Tolkien wrote in a 1937 letter to Father Christmas. But neither its surviving archive of papers, nor correspondence and recollections, allow its progress to be traced with certainty. It may have reached substantially its published form by the time Tolkien lent it to C.S. Lewis around the start of 1933, or it may be that its final chapters, with their greater seriousness and maturity of tone, were not composed until Allen & Unwin showed an interest in the work in 1936.

At any rate, Tolkien made a copy of *The Hobbit* suitable for lending, using his versatile Hammond typewriter which had compact, changeable fonts. He emended words and passages neatly in ink, and pasted corrected passages typed on slips precisely over earlier text. This 'home manuscript', as he called it, also contained versions of *Thror's Map* and a general map, *Wilderland*, as well as *Mirkwood* and an unknown number of other maps or illustrations. Between 1933 and 1936, Tolkien lent this reading copy to various friends and acquaintances, until at last, by some combination of events (again there are conflicting accounts), it came to the attention of Susan Dagnall, an assistant at George Allen & Unwin. Impressed by what she read, she convinced Tolkien that *The Hobbit* ought to be published. He took up the work, revised and finished the text, and on 3 October 1936 sent it to Allen & Unwin. Within two months it was accepted for publication and a contract was signed.

By then, production had already begun. On 28 November, Tolkien saw a specimen page and suggested changes to its design. Possibly at this time too he handed over five maps he planned to include with the text, which would have traced the journey of Bilbo Baggins eastward across wild lands to the Lonely Mountain and the lair of the dragon Smaug. These seem to have been, from extant sketches and correspondence, *Thror's Map*, *Wilderland*, a map of the Misty Mountains and the upper part of the Great River, one of the Lonely Mountain and surrounding lands, and one of the Long Lake combined with a view of the Lonely Mountain.

In drawing maps, however, Tolkien had used shading and multiple colours which could be printed only by the relatively expensive half-tone process. Susan Dagnall asked that he draw them again, with more careful lettering, to be reproduced by line-block. *Thror's Map* and *Wilderland* would be printed in only two colours, as endpapers, and the other three maps printed with the text in only one colour. (Definitions of the terms *half-tone* and *line-block* may be found near the end of this introduction.) In response, Tolkien made simpler versions of *Thror's Map* and *Wilderland*, hoping that these would serve even though he had, he said, 'small skill, and no experience of preparing such things for reproduction'; and he decided that the other maps were no longer needed, perhaps because he saw that *Wilderland* already contained most of their information.

In addition to the two revised maps, on 4 January 1937 Tolkien sent four illustrations for *The Hobbit* to Allen & Unwin. He had redrawn, he said, 'one or two of the amateur illustrations of the "home manuscript", conceiving that they might serve as endpapers, frontispiece or what not'. These were *Mirkwood*, *The Elvenking's Gate*, *Lake Town*, and *The Front Gate*. 'I think on the whole such things,' he wrote, 'if they were better, might be an improvement [to the volume as a whole]. But it may be impossible at this stage, and in any case they are not very good and may be technically unsuitable.' On the contrary, his publisher found the drawings admirable, and at once ordered blocks made for reproduction, though *Mirkwood* with its ink wash needed to be printed separately as a half-tone, and horizontal images (of these four, all except for *The Front Gate*) had to be turned parallel to the book's spine if they were not to be significantly reduced in size.

On 17 January, Tolkien sent Allen & Unwin six more illustrations: *The Hill: Hobbiton across the Water*, *The Trolls*, *The Mountain-path*, *The Misty Mountains Looking West from the Eyrie towards Goblin Gate*, *Beorn's Hall*, and *The Hall at Bag-End, Residence of B. Baggins Esquire*. 'They all are obviously defective,' he wrote, again with typical self-criticism, 'and quite apart from this may, each or some, present difficulties of reproduction.' He provided the further pictures, he said, because those he had sent earlier were, in subject matter, disproportionately concentrated towards the end of the story. He meant *The Hill* to come first among the illustrations, and *The Hall at Bag-End* last, beginning and ending the book with the 'quiet life' – that is, from Hobbiton 'one morning long ago in the quiet of the world' at the start of the tale, to the comfort of Bilbo's home in the final chapter.

Allen & Unwin had made no allowance for art in their budget, however, and did not dare to sell *The Hobbit*, a children's book, at more than a modest price. When Tolkien sent his first drawings, Susan Dagnall explained, 'they were so charming that we could not but insert them, although economically it was quite wrong to do so. And when you sent us the second batch we felt just the same!' But some economies had to be made. Although Tolkien wanted *Mirkwood* to be the front endpaper, and *Thror's Map* not only inserted in the text but with its secret runes or 'moon-letters' printed in mirror-reverse on the back of the sheet, so that they would be read correctly when the map was held up to the light (imitating the action of Elrond in chapter 3), Allen & Unwin decided that *Thror's Map* and *Wilderland*, each in two colours, had to be printed less expensively (on one side of a sheet) as endpapers rather than as part of the text or inserted as folded plates. In the event, the 'hidden' runes of *Thror's Map* were printed on its front, but in outline to suggest an ephemeral nature.

Such fine points at Allen & Unwin were in the capable hands of production manager Charles Furth. Along with Susan Dagnall, Furth corresponded with and visited Tolkien to ensure that proofs were corrected and other details seen to in a timely fashion. Long after the event, Rayner Unwin marvelled at the degree to which Furth and Dagnall indulged Tolkien and involved him in matters of design; but Tolkien had a keen eye for lettering and decoration, and there was precedent for successful author-illustrators of children's books, for instance in Hugh Lofting ('Doctor Dolittle') and Arthur Ransome ('Swallows and Amazons'). Thus Tolkien was invited, in February or March 1937, also to create a dust-jacket for *The Hobbit*. At this point, he was in the midst of correcting proofs for the book and making many alterations, to correct confusions of narrative and geography he had not noticed before. He could not design a jacket until this more urgent work was finished, but was able to supply a draft on 13 April and a revised jacket painting some two weeks later.

In May 1937, Allen & Unwin sent Tolkien sample binding cases for *The Hobbit* in different colours. He found them unattractive, and suggested that the binding could be improved with a small design of some kind, which he would try to produce. In July, after a delay due to illness, he submitted his own suggestion for a binding design, including runes and an 'ornamental dragon formula', and it was accepted.

The Hobbit was published by George Allen & Unwin on 21 September 1937. For the reader of that day, the scene was set while the book was still closed, by the trees and snow-capped mountains of Tolkien's wraparound dust-jacket art – or, if the jacket were removed, by the mountains, moons, suns, and winged dragons of the cloth binding, also a wraparound design. *Thror's Map* in black and red, made by Tolkien to look like an ancient 'artefact' and with its mysterious (Anglo-Saxon) runes, demanded attention as soon as the cover was opened to the front endsheet. Facing the title-page, then, was *The Hill: Hobbiton across the Water*. This and eight other black and white illustrations were printed by line-block at appropriate locations in the text, while *Mirkwood* was a separate half-tone inserted at the beginning of chapter 8 ('Flies and Spiders'). Finally, on the back endsheet, also in black and red, was the map *Wilderland*, extending from the 'Edge of the Wild' to the 'Desolation of Smaug'.

Altogether, *The Hobbit* offered a rich visual experience, in addition to the excitements of the text. To a large degree it still does, in standard editions including Tolkien's pictures, though his binding design has been abandoned (one of the dragon devices survives on the half-title), and as later printings became taller and narrower, the left and right edges of his dust-jacket art, with parts of a continuous runic border drawn for a trimmed paper size with different proportions, have been folded under with the flaps.

On 11 May 1937, Tolkien was informed that a firm in the U.S.A. was interested in publishing *The Hobbit*, but wanted to add four illustrations in colour by some good American artist. Charles Furth suggested instead that it would be best if all of the illustrations in *The Hobbit* were made by Tolkien himself. Tolkien replied on 13 May: 'I am divided between knowledge of my own inability and fear of what American artists (doubtless of admirable skill) might produce. In any case I agree that all the illustrations ought to be by the same hand: four professional pictures would make my own amateurish productions look rather silly.' By late July, he made four water-colour paintings for *The Hobbit*: *Rivendell, Bilbo Woke Up with the Early Sun in His Eyes, Bilbo Comes to the Huts of the Raft-elves*, and *Conversation with Smaug*. By 13 August, he completed a colour version of *The Hill*. The subjects of the paintings were chosen, he explained to Furth, so that they would be evenly distributed throughout the book. *The Hill: Hobbiton-across-the Water* was based directly on the original frontispiece, and trials survive for *Rivendell* and *Bilbo Comes to the Huts of the Raft-elves* – these are reproduced below (figs. 18–22 and 104, 60–63 and 105) – but there are no extant preliminary drawings, if there ever were any, for *Bilbo Woke Up* or *Conversation with Smaug*.

The five colour pictures, among the finest work Tolkien achieved as an artist, were produced too late to be used in the first printing of *The Hobbit* by Allen & Unwin. Four of them, however, were added to the second Allen & Unwin printing (dated 1937, not published until January 1938), all except for *Bilbo Woke Up with the Early Sun in His Eyes*. Tolkien marvelled that Allen & Unwin were able to include four additional pictures, in colour, without having to raise the price of the book. The American publisher, the Houghton Mifflin Company, likewise took four of the water-colours, including *Bilbo Woke Up* but not *Bilbo Comes to the Huts of the Raft-elves*, but printed them cropped or masked, in particular without their integral title panels. Only later were all of the *Hobbit* paintings included, complete, in the British and American editions. Houghton Mifflin also had an unknown artist redraw *Mirkwood* without shading, so that it could be printed as a line-block rather than an inserted half-tone, and to fit a wider page size, extended *Thror's Map* and *Wilderland* at left and right. The endpaper maps were then printed entirely in red, rather than black and red, and inserted in the wrong order.

Finding the Allen & Unwin dust-jacket art too 'British', Houghton Mifflin chose for its edition of *The Hobbit* to print *The Hill: Hobbiton-across-the Water* on the upper jacket panel, and on the lower panel *Conversation with Smaug*. Tolkien found the result appalling: both paintings were set within bright blue and red frames, and were partly obscured by advertising blurbs printed across them. Houghton Mifflin adopted Tolkien's jacket art with their second edition of *The Hobbit* (1951), and still use it today on some of their printings; but they have preferred a simpler cloth binding, without Tolkien's decorative design.

For the most part, early reviewers of *The Hobbit*, when they mentioned its art, did so with favour, praising Tolkien for his fanciful, thrilling, even 'knobbly' and 'niggling' (but also 'eerie') illustrations, and for his attention to detail and consistency. Only much later was it noted how the pictures, no less than the text, serve to draw the reader into the world of *The Hobbit*. The critic Margery Fisher has said that while Tolkien's illustrations 'are not self-consciously naïve, they put into visual form the kind of magic world which a child might well have imagined'. Fisher also observed that when he appears in the *Hobbit* art, the figure of Bilbo varies in size: at home, in *The Hall at Bag-End*, he is 'normal', but on all other occasions – next to the great eagle in *Bilbo Woke Up with the Early Sun in His Eyes*, riding a barrel on the river in *Bilbo Comes to the Huts of the Raft-elves*, or bowing respectfully to a huge dragon in a cave piled high with treasure in *Conversation with Smaug* – he is minute in relation to his surroundings. Tolkien, she wrote, in his pictures underlined 'what is obvious in the story – Bilbo's diminutive size and sheer ordinariness'. Just so; but because Tolkien had limited skill in drawing the human (or hobbit) figure, it was to his advantage to keep Bilbo small, partly concealed, or in silhouette. It is also worth noting that the men in *Lake Town* are similarly miniaturized, and that Tolkien chose not to publish earlier finished illustrations for *The Hobbit* which contained figures, having been advised, as he told Charles Furth, that those pictures 'with a geographical or landscape content were the most suitable' for the book, 'even apart from my inability to draw anything else'.

In the 'home manuscript' of *The Hobbit*, Tolkien could be unapologetically an amateur artist. He could draw what he liked, and choose whichever medium was convenient or suited his mood: graphite, ink, coloured pencil, or paint. In this context, friends and members of his family who saw his work would likely overlook any lack of polish in a picture. But a printed book may reach many readers, most of them unknown to the author and each a potential critic. Tolkien's concern to produce art to a higher standard for the published *Hobbit* is clear in many of his letters to Allen & Unwin and in the effort he put into his final illustrations. For some of his *Hobbit* pictures, Tolkien reached their final form only after making numerous trial sketches. Good examples of this process are his views of Hobbiton (*The Hill*) and of the entrance to the Elvenking's halls. Sometimes, he borrowed elements from pictures he had made earlier: *Mirkwood*, for instance, was adapted from his view of Taur-nu-Fuin; a dragon for *Thror's Map* came from a small picture inspired by *Beowulf*; another dragon was used earlier in an illustration for *Roverandom*; and the lines of trees in the foreground of the *Hobbit* dust-jacket bear a close resemblance to those in his painting *The Wood at the World's End*. Tolkien also looked to the work of professional artists for inspiration: *The Trolls* is almost certainly based on a picture by Jennie Harbour for the story of Hansel and Gretel, and *Bilbo Woke Up with the Early Sun in His Eyes* includes, from a book on birds, a Golden Eagle originally drawn by Alexander Thorburn.

In truth, literature as engaging as *The Hobbit* does not need illustrations. But when the author himself has provided the art, and is a talented illustrator of his own work, it should be particularly welcome to the reader, for whom it opens new dimensions to an already excellent story. One of the writers of the present book first came upon *The Hobbit* in an edition without illustrations, and for years did not know how much poorer he was without the addition of Tolkien's art to Tolkien's words. *The Art of The Hobbit by J.R.R. Tolkien* displays all of the illustrations produced by Tolkien for one of his best-loved stories, in so far as they are known to his family and scholars. We have also included a few pictures he drew for other purposes but which influenced his *Hobbit* art.

~

In our comments we use two terms common to the printing trade at the time *The Hobbit* was first published, and which it may be useful to define for today's reader. *Line-block* and *half-tone* were processes by which art was transferred by means of photography onto metal (usually zinc) plates; these were then etched in acid, leaving the design in relief. In 1937, books were commonly printed with metal type, itself a relief medium, and relief plates could be printed in the same press. The *line-block* was used for art composed of solid lines or dots, such as Tolkien's drawings in pen and ink. The *half-tone* was used for shaded art, such as *Mirkwood*, which was photographed through a screen to break the image into dots; when printed, this kind of plate gave the illusion of tone. For the best quality of reproduction, half-tones were usually printed on smooth coated paper. Tolkien's water-colour illustrations were also printed as half-tones, but with multiple blocks, created with filters which separated the art into its colour components (tones of red, blue, and yellow) as well as black.

For the most part, we have reproduced Tolkien's pictures as large as possible, but with margins wide enough to give the art presence and provide room for captions. In only a few instances is an image larger than its original size (and then not much larger); and, except for the details collected as figs. 59 and 103, we have avoided the enlargement of pictures which in the original are very small, so as to present them honestly and without distortion. Although we have aimed throughout for accuracy of colour, some sketches have been darkened to show faint pencil-work. There are natural variations in background tones – Tolkien used a variety of papers, often whatever was at hand, including lined writing paper – and we have had to compensate for variations in image quality from different sources.

Except for *Mirkwood*, which has been lost, the reproductions in this book have been made from the original art, thus showing in many cases pencil sketching under ink or paint, and sometimes corrections in white paint – features invisible to the high-contrast copy camera in creating line-blocks for printing, but which are important to anyone who would study the pictorial development of *The Hobbit* from its beginnings in manuscript to its appearance as a printed book. On occasion, the reproductions also contain reference numbers added to the Tolkien papers, or portions of archival tapes used to bind the art within albums.

For quotations from *The Hobbit*, we have used the most accurate current text (*The Annotated Hobbit*, 2002) except where otherwise noted. And although we give some details of the story of *The Hobbit* in our comments on the art, we have necessarily assumed that our readers are already familiar with Tolkien's book.

A more extensive history of *The Hobbit* may be found in our *J.R.R. Tolkien Companion and Guide* (2006). Readers also may be interested in *The Annotated Hobbit*, edited by Douglas A. Anderson (revised edition, 2002), which includes many illustrations for *The Hobbit* by artists other than Tolkien; *The History of The Hobbit* by John D. Rateliff (2007, revised 2011); and our *J.R.R. Tolkien: Artist and Illustrator* (1995).

Tolkien's correspondence with George Allen & Unwin has been quoted, for the most part, directly from the archive currently held by HarperCollins U.K. (successor to Allen & Unwin), though much of it is also published in *The Letters of J.R.R. Tolkien* (1981). Rayner Unwin's comment about Allen & Unwin indulging Tolkien was made in his memoir, *George Allen & Unwin: A Remembrancer* (1999). The unsigned review by C.S. Lewis, 'A World for Children', appeared in the *Times Literary Supplement* for 2 October 1937 on p. 714. Margery Fisher's comments on *The Hobbit* are contained in 'An Old Favourite', published in *Growing Point* for December 1976, p. 3014. Christopher Tolkien's words about Nargothrond, quoted on p.83, appear in his foreword to the 50th anniversary edition of *The Hobbit* (Unwin Hyman, 1987).

Wayne G. Hammond & Christina Scull

The Art of THE HOBBIT
by J.R.R. Tolkien

1. *One Morning Early in the Quiet of the World*

Bag-End Underhill

One Morning Early in the Quiet of the World (fig. 1) shows the arrival of Gandalf at Bag-End, 'one morning long ago in the quiet of the world, when there was less noise and more green. . . . Bilbo Baggins was standing at his door after breakfast smoking an enormous long wooden pipe that reached nearly down to his woolly toes (neatly brushed)' (ch. 1). Although sketched roughly and very small (see fig. 103 for a larger reproduction), the figure of Bilbo corresponds to Tolkien's description of Hobbits in chapter 1: 'a little people, about half our height', 'inclined to be fat in the stomach', curly-haired, and wearing no shoes. In the middle distance, beyond the chimney smoke of a neighbour of Bag-End, is a view towards the region of Hobbit country called the Westfarthing in *The Lord of the Rings*. The angular pencil mark above the horizon, shaped like an eagle's beak, may be no more than a sideways sketch of Gandalf's hat.

In Bilbo's hobbit-hole, 'the best rooms were all on the left-hand side (going in), for these were the only ones to have windows, deep-set round windows looking over his garden, and meadows beyond, sloping down to the river' (ch. 1). But in the early picture *Bag End Underhill* (fig. 2), when Tolkien was still working out the 'architecture' of Bag-End, he tentatively drew windows on the right-hand side of the door as well. Above the entrance is a large tree, in later drawings moved to the top of the hill. Bilbo's door is approached between tall shrubs growing in pots, and beside it is the bench on which Bilbo sits to talk with Gandalf.

Gandalf (fig. 3) accurately depicts the wizard as 'a little old man with a tall pointed blue hat, a long grey cloak, a silver scarf over which his long white beard hung down below his waist, and immense black boots', carrying a pointed staff (ch. 1, 1937 text). He stands next to the entrance to Bag-End, 'a perfectly round door like a porthole, painted green, with a shiny yellow brass knob in the exact middle' and a bell-pull at the side. The finished drawing at the centre, within faintly sketched lines of the hill, also shows the runic marks scratched by Gandalf on Bilbo's door, which the dwarf Gloin will read as *Burglar wants a good job, plenty of Excitement and reasonable Reward.*

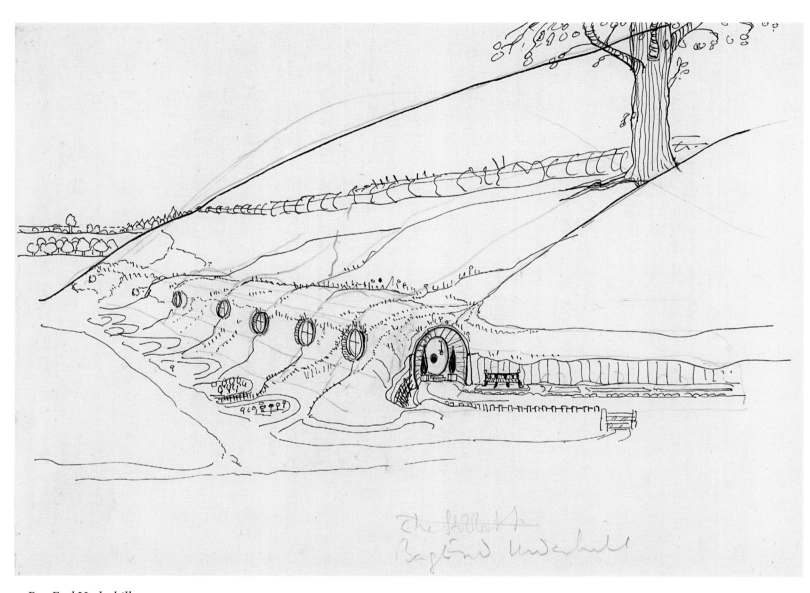

2. *Bag End Underhill*

3. *Gandalf*

The Hill: Hobbiton

In chapter 2 of *The Hobbit*, having been rushed out of his comfortable home by Gandalf, Bilbo runs 'as fast as his furry feet could carry him down the lane, past the great Mill, across The Water, and then on for a mile or more' to meet the dwarf Thorin Oakenshield and his companions. Tolkien illustrated this route from Bag-End down to The Water – the stream beside The Mill – in a series of preliminary and finished pictures of The Hill and part of the village of Hobbiton.

Bilbo's home is near the top of *The Hill: Hobbiton* (fig. 4), drawn as in *Bag End Underhill* (fig. 2) but without the large tree and now showing more fully the adjacent garden and meadows. Here that 'most luxurious hobbit-hole . . . to be found either under The Hill or over The Hill or across The Water' (ch. 1) is set well apart from other dwellings. A signpost at lower left points up the lane to Bag-End, suggesting its importance in the neighbourhood. Other holes are shown at upper right, and more traditional houses and outbuildings in the middle ground. Tolkien took special pains in drawing The Mill, with detailed stonework, shingles, a weathervane, and a churning stream: in the manuscript of *The Hobbit*, Bilbo met the dwarves at 'the Great Mill' rather than, as published, at the Green Dragon Inn, Bywater.

An untitled picture (fig. 5) has the same long, winding path, but with new hobbit-holes and tall trees on the upper lane almost obscuring Bag-End. On the other side of the same sheet is a second drawing entitled *The Hill: Hobbiton* (fig. 6), with holes dug into the bank of the lane and, most notably, a bridge at the bottom edge, which Bilbo crosses in the published text.

In other drawings, Tolkien experimented further with the curve of the lane and the location of trees and buildings. He also redesigned The Mill, pointing its extension to the east (right) rather than the west, and he developed the fields below Bag-End. Apparently dissatisfied with the tight perspective of fig. 7, he abandoned it as no more than a quick sketch. In fig. 8, the lane appears to be so steep that Bilbo's dash down the hill would have been perilous, while in fig. 9 it is like a writhing snake. Eventually, Tolkien struck a more pleasing balance.

4. *The Hill: Hobbiton*

5. The Hill: Hobbiton

The first finished result of these sketches was *The Hill: Hobbiton across the Water* (fig. 10). It contains a wealth of detail, from the door of Bag-End to the three birds scratching in the yard behind The Mill. Open fields are divided by fences and hedgerows. Furrows and haystacks speak of a farming culture. Shadows cast beneath trees and across the lane suggest bright sunlight. The sky, empty in earlier drawings of Hobbiton, is now filled with drifting clouds, while another, more distant land of trees and hills is glimpsed at upper left. The picture is signed (at lower left), as are others for *The Hobbit*, with Tolkien's 'JRRT' monogram.

This ink drawing appeared, opposite the title-page, only in the first British printing of *The Hobbit*, issued in September 1937. Too late for this printing but in time for the second, Tolkien completed *The Hill: Hobbiton-across-the Water* (fig. 11), one of five colour illustrations wanted by his American publisher, and this was substituted for the black and white frontispiece. Although based on a tracing of the earlier work, the painting is a further development. Most of the rectangular windows shown in the ink version, notably in The Mill, are now round as at Bag-End, and the signpost points more generally to the 'Hill'. Moreover, the availability of colour allowed Tolkien to show Hobbiton and Bag-End in bright sunshine under a blue sky on a cheerful spring day, with gardens in full bloom. It is an idyllic place which Bilbo is reluctant to leave, and to which he naturally longs to return when in wild lands far to the east.

Most of the details in both the ink and water-colour versions of *The Hill* are not described in *The Hobbit*, but came to feature in *The Lord of the Rings*, where the Shire (as the larger Hobbit country is named in the later book) itself plays an important role in the story. Just below Bag-End are the field and Party Tree where Bilbo celebrates his 'eleventy-first' birthday. The three hobbit-holes to the south of Bilbo's gardens comprise Bagshot Row, where Sam Gamgee lives with his father. The buildings at the centre of the picture are the Old Grange, and the trees nearby (though this is clear only in the water-colour) are the chestnuts cut down by order of Saruman. The Mill is that owned by Ted Sandyman's father. The distant landscape is, perhaps, Bindbole Wood in the Northfarthing, described in *The Hobbit* only as the land 'over The Hill'.

The Hill: Hobbiton across the Water.

10. *The Hill: Hobbiton across the Water*

The hill : hobbiton~across~the Water

11. *The Hill: Hobbiton-across-the Water*

A Letter to Bilbo

In the morning after the 'unexpected party', Bilbo receives a letter left for him on his mantelpiece, 'just under the clock' (ch. 2):

> *Thorin and Company to Burglar Bilbo greeting! For your hospitality our sincerest thanks, and for your offer of professional assistance our grateful acceptance. Terms: cash on delivery, up to and not exceeding one fourteenth of total profits (if any); all travelling expenses guaranteed in any event; funeral expenses to be defrayed by us or our representatives, if occasion arises and the matter is not otherwise arranged for.*
>
> > *Thinking it unnecessary to disturb your esteemed repose, we have proceeded in advance to make requisite preparations, and shall await your respected person at the Green Dragon Inn, Bywater, at 11 a.m. sharp. Trusting that you will be punctual,*
> > > *We have the honour to remain*
> > > *Yours deeply*
> > > *Thorin & Co.*

Tolkien imagined this message written (on Bilbo's 'own note-paper') in English, but in the 'Elvish' script *tengwar*, which he had invented in relation to his 'Silmarillion' mythology; and he could not resist making a private 'facsimile' (fig. 12). The handwriting is meant to be Thorin's, deliberately bold to match his personality. In a letter to the newspaper *The Observer*, 20 February 1938, Tolkien commented that Dwarves at times used *tengwar*, as 'in the curse inscribed on the pot of gold in the picture of Smaug's lair' (*Conversation with Smaug*, fig. 71).

That the facsimile of Bilbo's contract with the dwarves was a late production is clear from its mention of 'the Green Dragon Inn', which replaced 'the Great Mill' in the *Hobbit* text only in page proof. Two other versions of the letter-contract in *tengwar* survive among Tolkien's papers, in texts which explain that the Dwarves used runes only for special purposes, while for ordinary writing they preferred the Elvish alphabet.

12. Thorin's letter to Bilbo

13. *Trolls' Hill*

The Trolls

On a cold, wet evening, 'the wind broke up the grey clouds, and a wandering moon appeared above the hills between the flying rags'. Bilbo and the dwarves, now 'far into the Lone-lands', see 'a hill some way off with trees on it, pretty thick in parts. Out of the dark mass of the trees they could now see a light shining, a reddish comfortable-looking light, as it might be a fire or torches twinkling' (ch. 2). This is the view that Tolkien depicts in *Trolls' Hill* (fig. 13), with a flash of red flame at centre left.

Bilbo, the 'burglar', investigates the light, and is caught by three trolls. The dwarves are also taken, when they look for Bilbo, and are 'neatly tied up in sacks'. In his text, Tolkien leaves the trolls to his readers' imagination, saying only that they are 'very large' and 'fair-sized'. But in two illustrations, both entitled *The Three Trolls Are Turned to Stone* (figs. 14, 15), he shows them in full figure, along with the paraphernalia of their camp, some of the dwarves in sacks, and the face of Bilbo peering out of the foliage at upper left. The second of these pictures is a more carefully drawn version of the first. In both, the trolls are in the open as dawn breaks and they turn to stone – 'for trolls, as you probably know, must be underground before dawn, or they go back to the stuff of the mountains they are made of'. At right is the figure of Gandalf, stepping out from behind a tree and raising his staff.

It may be that Tolkien was unhappy with the figures in *The Three Trolls Are Turned to Stone*, or knew that the ink wash he had used would not reproduce well by line-block. In any case, he drew a new picture for publication, *The Trolls* (fig. 16). A 'very large fire of beech-logs' is burning at the centre. The three trolls are hiding just beyond the light, waiting for the dwarves to come one by one into the circle of trees; one dwarf is approaching at the bottom of the picture. Light, shadow, and twisting smoke and flame create a stunning effect.

The basic composition of *The Trolls* was inspired by an illustration by Jennie Harbour for the story of Hansel and Gretel, contained in a book of fairy-tales owned by Priscilla Tolkien (see *J.R.R. Tolkien: Artist and Illustrator*, fig. 101). But Tolkien's picture is more stylized and evokes a greater sense of menace.

. The Three Trolls are turned to Stone .

14. *The Three Trolls Are Turned to Stone,* first version

The Three Trolls are turned to Stone

15. *The Three Trolls Are Turned to Stone,* second version

.The Trolls.

16. *The Trolls*

Rivendell

At 'the very edge of the Wild' the travellers find rest among the elves of Rivendell, where Elrond lives in 'the Last Homely House west of the Mountains' (ch. 3). On the slopes of this fair valley are stands of pine, beech, and oak. 'Hurrying water' flowing through 'a rocky bed' is spanned by 'a narrow bridge of stone'. Although *The Hobbit* makes it clear that the valley of Rivendell is remarkably deep – Bilbo and company reach its floor by a 'steep zig-zag path' – in the picture *Riding Down into Rivendell* (fig. 17) only the line of treetops along the river suggests that the path descends far below the level of Gandalf and his horse. On the far side of the bridge is a large house with a portico (or porch) supported by five columns.

On the other side of this sheet is an alternate drawing of the house (fig. 18), with many windows and a longer portico with eight columns. In place of a central tower as in *Riding Down into Rivendell* there seems to be an open courtyard, with a chimney at each of the four corners of the surrounding structure. Yet another, very quick sketch of the Last Homely House (fig. 19) has five columns and a distinctly classical appearance, with formal steps along the entire width of the entrance.

Despite its title, *Rivendell Looking West* (fig. 20) is a view to the east. Tolkien added the words 'Looking West' to the original title *Rivendell* at some later date, possibly noticing only his sketch of Elrond's house at bottom centre and concluding that, since the house is north of the river (as shown on the map *Wilderland*, figs. 88, 89), the orientation of the picture must be to the west. But the river flows out of the Misty Mountains from the east, and close inspection of the art reveals another sketch of a house, in the correct position, at lower left. The great depth and steepness of the valley are now dramatically apparent. (See also fig. 104.)

Rivendell Looking East (fig. 21), also at first simply *Rivendell*, likewise shows a deep valley, but with a wide vista of fields, hills, and distant peaks. Tolkien obviously spent a great deal of time with this much more elaborate and more finished picture, using coloured pencil to build multiple textures into the tall cliffs. The house again has a tower, as well as a fenced enclosure. Unique to this view is a heavy bridge with three arches spanning a wider river.

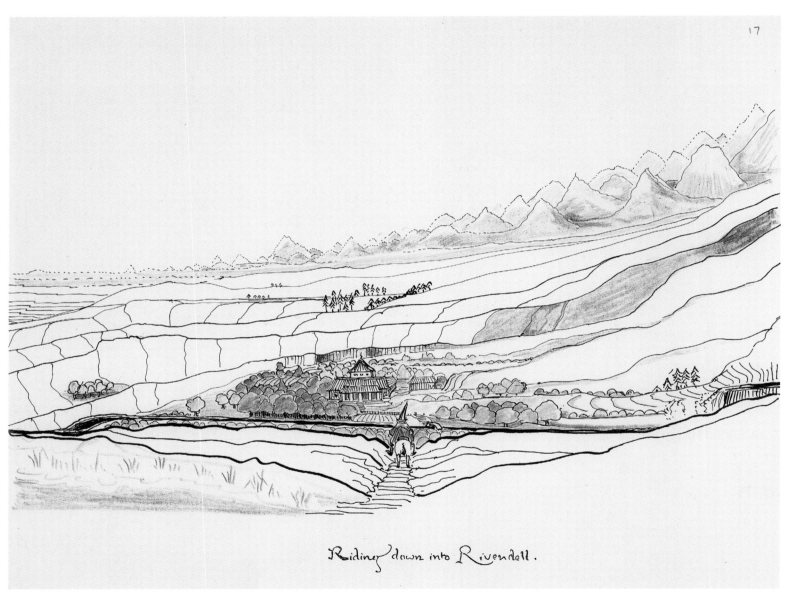

Riding down into Rivendell.

17. *Riding Down into Rivendell*

Thror's Map

The first sketch of *Thror's Map* appears on one of only six pages to survive from the earliest manuscript of *The Hobbit* (fig. 24). Strictly speaking, at its making it was 'Fimbulfambi's map', as the dwarf later called Thror was named at the time. Douglas A. Anderson in *The Annotated Hobbit* identifies the symbols at the compass points as the constellation Ursa Major (North), the Sun (South), and possibly, from 'The Silmarillion', the Gates of Morn (East) and the Mountains of Valinor (West). The runic inscription below the sinister hand reads: FANG THE SECRET PASSAGE OF THE DWARVES. Below that are draft and revised inscriptions for the visible runes and the hidden 'moon-letters' Tolkien would use for later versions of the map (as published, 'five feet high the door and three may walk abreast', with the initials of Thror and Thrain, and 'stand by the grey stone when the thrush knocks and the setting sun with the last light of Durin's Day will shine upon the key-hole'). By the mountain, an F-rune (which it seems reasonable to think stands for 'Fang') marks the secret door, and 'F G' the front gate. The dwarves' first camp (in chapter 11) is marked in lighter ink just west of the southern spur. At lower right is a sketch of the Lonely Mountain similar to the drawing in fig. 87.

On the later *Thror's Map. Copied by B. Baggins* (fig. 25), the pencilled words by Tolkien at the top are the text of the visible runes translated into his invented language Noldorin, while those at the bottom are the same text in Old English. The compass points are now simply the runes for N, E, S, and W, while the secret door is marked with the rune for D. The titling at lower left suggests that the drawing was meant to be an 'artefact', a copy made by Bilbo from the 'real' dwarves' map; and it is in this form that Tolkien wanted it inserted in *The Hobbit*, either at the first mention of the map in chapter 1 or when it is examined further in chapter 3. This is, in fact, a more direct rendering of the 'plan of the Mountain' described in the first chapter, with the dragon marked in red on the mountain rather than beside it as in the published art. The 'secret' moon-letters written on the other side of the sheet (see fig. 30) are meant to be read by holding the sheet up to a light, thus simulating the effect of the runes as they are revealed to Elrond.

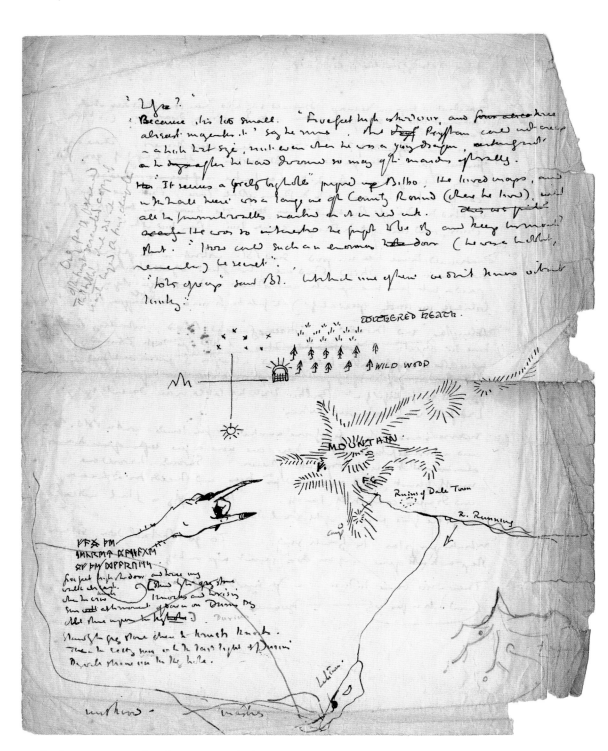

24. Early manuscript for chapter 1, with sketch of *Thror's Map*

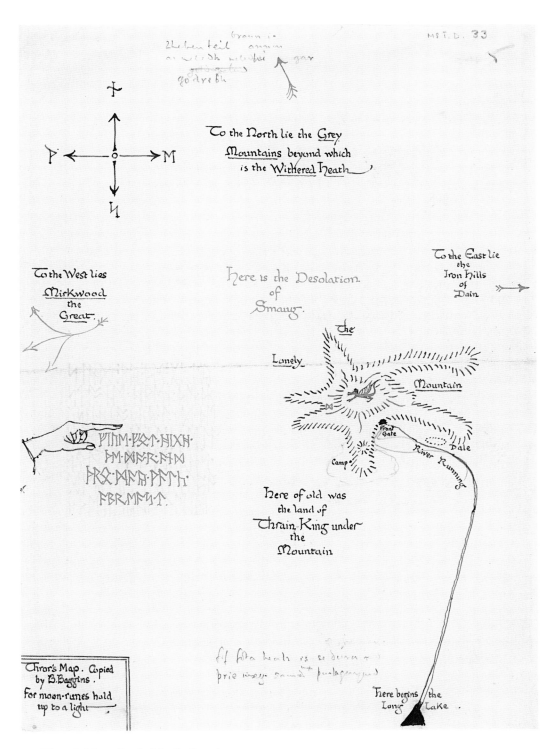

To the North lie the Grey
Mountains beyond which
is the Withered Heath

To the East lie
the
Iron hills
of
Dain

To the West lies
Mirkwood
the
Great.

Here is the Desolation
of
Smaug.

the

Lonely

Mountain

Front
Gate

Dale

River Running

Camp

Here of old was
the land of
Thrain King under
the
Mountain

Here begins the
Long Lake.

Thror's Map. Copied
by B. Baggins.
For moon-runes hold
up to a light

25. *Thror's Map. Copied by B. Baggins*

51

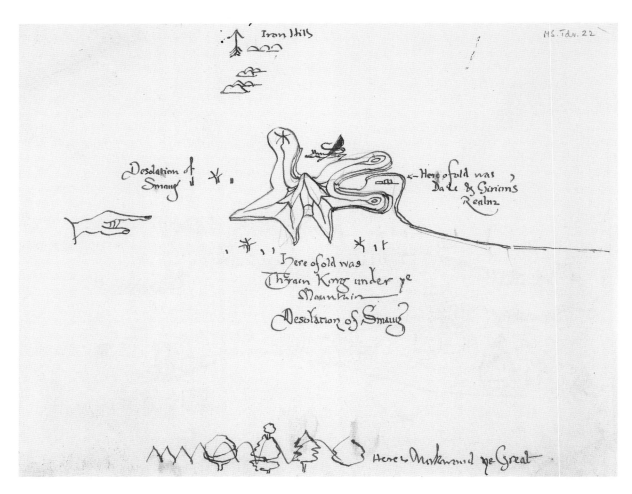

Iron Hills

MS. Tdw. 22

Desolation of
Smaug

→ Here of old was
Dale & Girions
Realm

Here of old was
Thrain King under ye
Mountain

Desolation of Smaug

Here is Mirkwud ye Great

26. Sketch for *Thror's Map*

27. Dragon and warrior

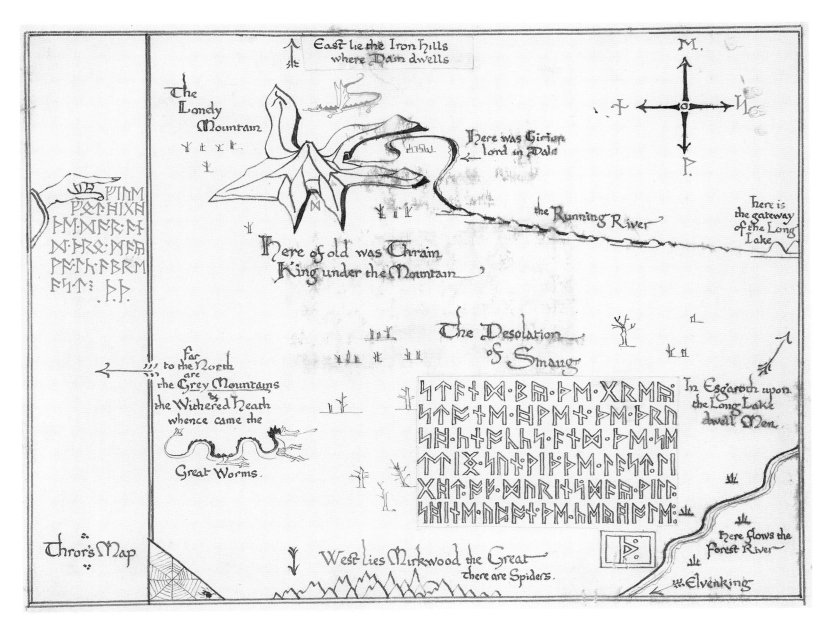

East lie the Iron hills
where Dáin dwells

The Lonely Mountain

Here was Girion
lord in Dale

the Running River

Here is the gateway of the Long Lake

Here of old was Thrain
King under the Mountain

The Desolation of Smaug

far to the North
are the Grey Mountains
& the Withered Heath
whence came the

Great Worms.

In Esgaroth upon the Long Lake dwell Men.

Thror's Map

West lies Mirkwood the Great
there are Spiders.

Here flows the Forest River

Elvenking

28. *Thror's Map* final art (with alterations)

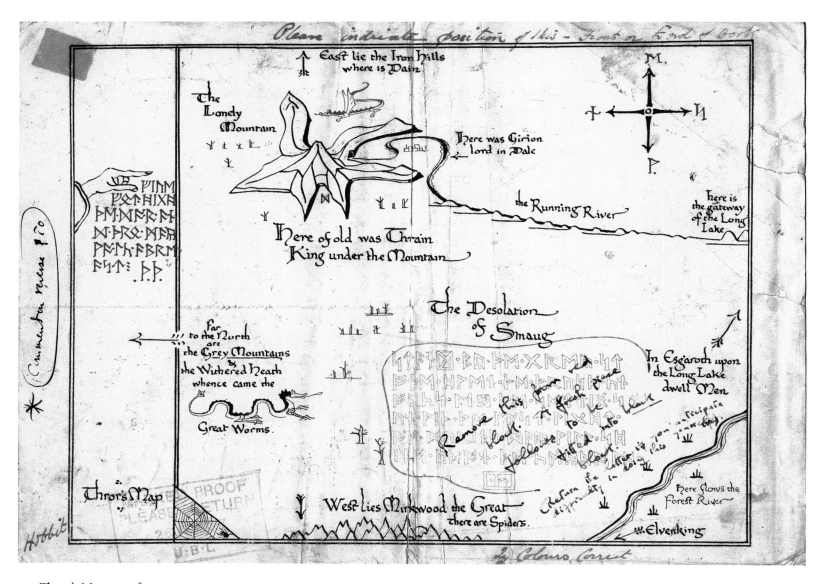

29. *Thror's Map* proof

Matters of cost, however, required that *Thror's Map* appear as an endpaper, with the moon-runes visible on the front (as they had to be, with the back pasted down). Tolkien drew at least one sketch for a new version, notably adding a wide bend to the river around Dale and with 'Desolation of Smaug' labelled twice (fig. 26). In the finished art (fig. 28) East is now at the top: a result of turning the image ninety degrees, but also a common feature of medieval maps, which *Thror's Map* resembles with its rudimentary drawing and lettering. (In a preface to the 1966 edition of *The Hobbit*, Tolkien explained that having East at the top was 'usual in dwarf-maps'.) For the 'great worm' at lower left, he borrowed a dragon he had drawn in an unrelated picture (fig. 27). When Allen & Unwin tried to suggest the ephemeral nature of the 'moon-letters' by printing them in light red (as in the proof, fig. 29), Tolkien asked that they appear instead in black and without the tint effect. He also wished to replace the moon-letters with redrawn runes, and the words at top with a revision ('East lie the Iron Hills where Dain dwells'), and to this end pasted new lettering onto the original art; but Allen & Unwin were not able to make these changes to the published map, which still includes the earlier moon-runes and the legend 'East lie the Iron Hills where is Dain'.

In *The Hobbit* Tolkien represented dwarf-runes with those used in Anglo-Saxon England. The main block of runes in fig. 30, on the back of the sheet containing *Thror's Map. Copied by B. Baggins* (fig. 25), is the text of the moon-letters in mirror-reverse. Tolkien referred to that map when drawing his final version, and possibly at that time scribbled rough translations of the hidden runes into Noldorin, Old Norse, and Old English, together with the text in Modern English. Near the top is also the text of the visible runes, but written out in a runic alphabet of Tolkien's own development rather than in English runes.

There are several drawings of the moon-letters among Tolkien's papers, made with single strokes or in outline (figs. 31, 32), straightforward or in mirror-reverse. The TH-rune at end stands for 'Thror'. The runes used on the published map (fig. 33) were drawn by Tolkien on the back of the final art (fig. 28) and made into a separate line-block by Allen & Unwin. At some point, the sheet containing *Thror's Map* became damp, causing some of the ink to run on both sides.

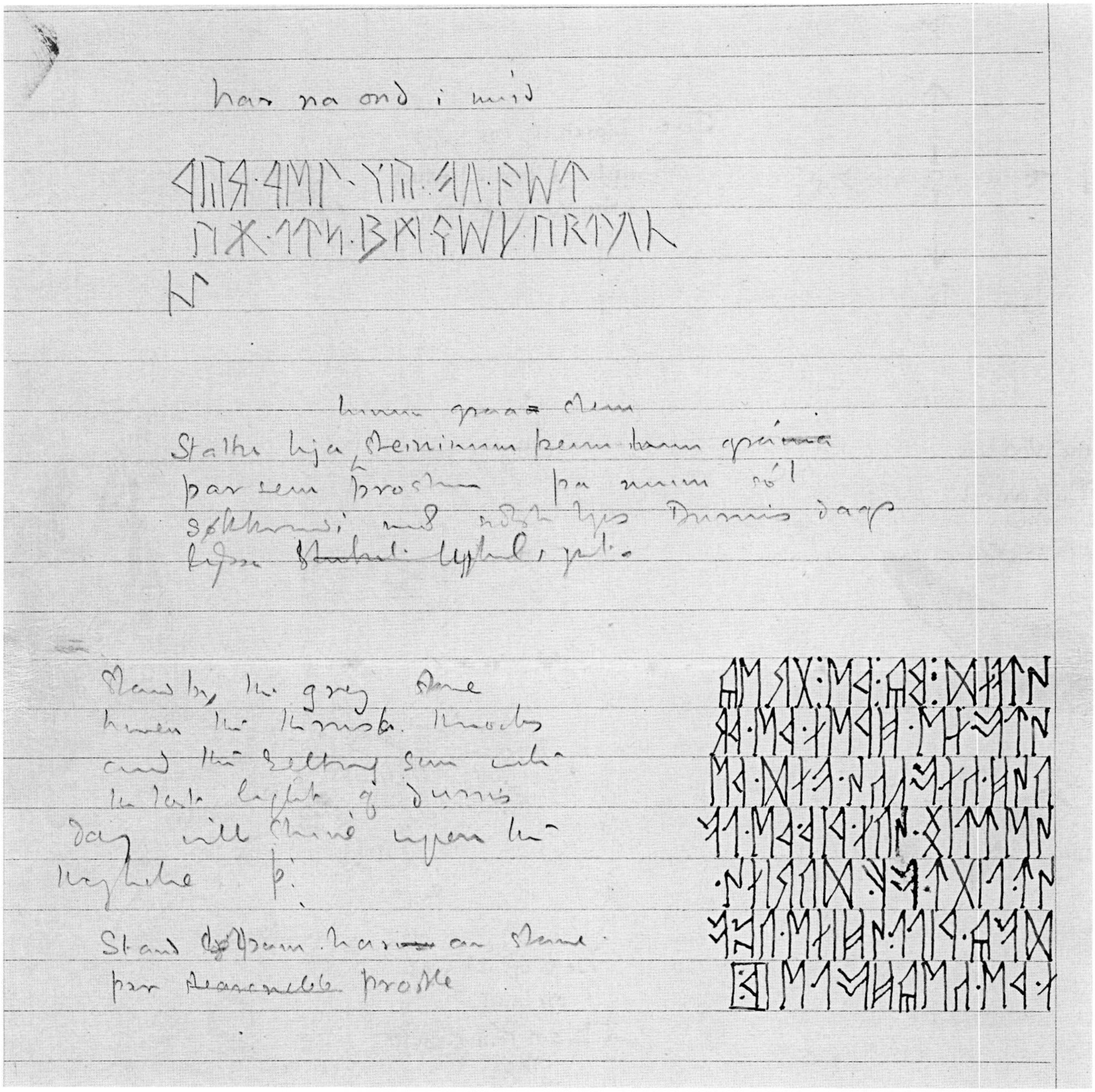

30. Sketches for moon-letters

31, 32. Moon-letters drawn in mirror-reverse

33. *These Are the Moon Runes Seen by Elrond*

34. *The Mountain-path*

The Misty Mountains

Leaving behind the Last Homely House, Bilbo and his companions travel over, and under, 'great tall mountains with lonely peaks and valleys' (ch. 4). Tolkien included many of these in his *Hobbit* art, and for his pictures of the Misty Mountains as for those of Rivendell, his model was the Swiss Alps. As he wrote long after the event: 'The hobbit's (Bilbo's) journey from Rivendell to the other side of the Misty Mountains, including the glissade down the slithering stones into the pine woods, is based on my adventures in 1911.' A thunderstorm experienced in Switzerland influenced the 'thunder-battle' in chapter 4, which Tolkien depicted in *The Mountain-path* (fig. 34): 'The lightning splinters on the peaks, and rocks shiver, and great crashes split the air and go rolling and tumbling into every cave and hollow; and the darkness is filled with overwhelming noise and sudden light.'

By the time he came to illustrate *The Hobbit*, Tolkien had drawn spectacular mountain landscapes associated with 'The Silmarillion', most notably *Halls of Manwë on the Mountains of the World above Faerie*, better known as *Taniquetil* (see *J.R.R. Tolkien: Artist and Illustrator*, fig. 52). In the lines of its stony heights, that painting of the greatest of mountains has a visual analogue in a slightly later, untitled landscape (fig. 36), perhaps another memory of Switzerland, in which a narrow road runs past tulip-shaped trees and through a pine-wood at the base of tall, narrow peaks. Tolkien was a frugal artist, occasionally reusing parts of one picture in another; and so this image found expression again, with similar mountains and stylized trees, in the ink drawing *The Misty Mountains Looking West from the Eagles' Eyrie towards Goblin Gate* (fig. 37).

For publication, Tolkien redrew this picture with more natural trees and contour lines. *The Misty Mountains Looking West from the Eyrie towards Goblin Gate* (fig. 38), like the previous version, is a bird's-eye view from the 'wide shelf of rock on the mountainside' to which Bilbo, Gandalf, and the dwarves are taken by the eagles in chapter 6, and shows the gate through which Bilbo escapes from the Goblin caves by a shaded semi-circle. Although a horizontal image, in the first edition it was not turned sideways, but much reduced on the page.

35. *The Misty Mountains*

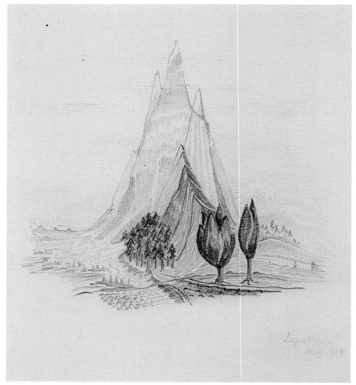

36. Mountain landscape

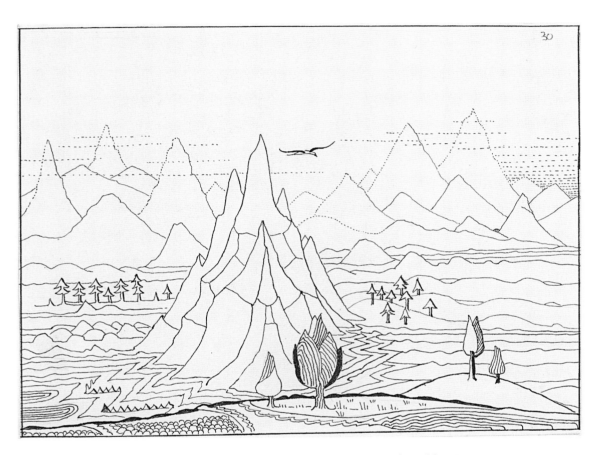

37. *The Misty Mountains Looking West from the Eagles' Eyrie towards Goblin Gate*

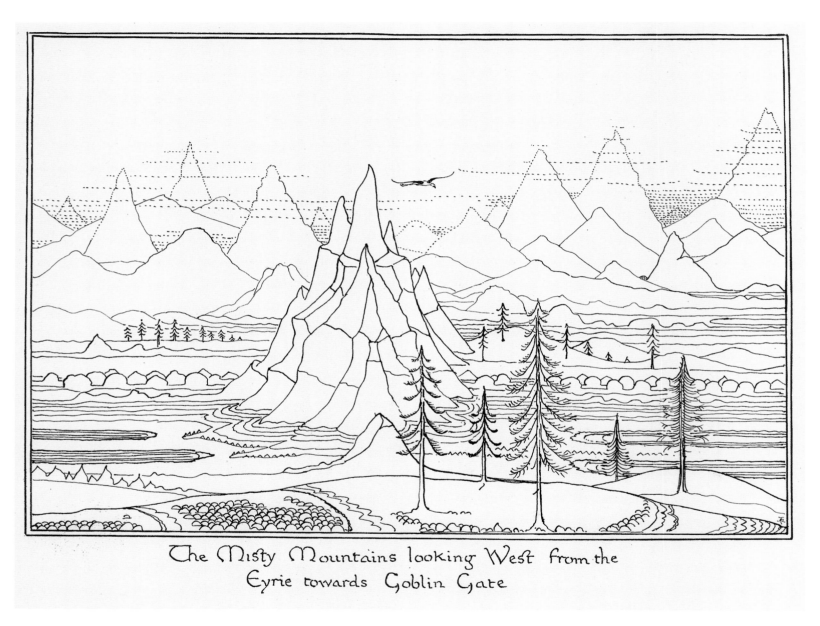

The Misty Mountains looking West from the Eyrie towards Goblin Gate

38. *The Misty Mountains Looking West from the Eyrie towards Goblin Gate*

39. *Bilbo Woke Up with the Early Sun in His Eyes*

40. *Eagles' Eyrie*

64

In *Bilbo Woke Up with the Early Sun in His Eyes* (fig. 39), it is the morning after the hobbit has been rescued from the goblins and wargs. Golden sunlight shines upon the land, while 'mists were in the valleys and hollows and twined here and there about the peaks and pinnacles of the hills' (ch. 7). The enormous size of the standing eagle may be gauged in relation to the figure of Bilbo, who, according to a statement Tolkien made to his American publisher, would be 'about three feet or three feet six inches' in height – although Tolkien did not always draw Bilbo correctly to scale. He based his great eagle, with stylized, almost metallic feathers, on a picture derived from one of an immature Golden Eagle painted by Alexander Thorburn for Lord Lilford's *Birds of the British Islands* (1891).

A curious feature of *Bilbo Woke Up* is that the hobbit is wearing black boots, though there is no mention in the text that he acquired them. 'There should be!' Tolkien remarked. 'It has dropped out somehow or other in the various revisions – the bootings occurred at Rivendell, and [Bilbo] was again bootless after leaving Rivendell on the way home. But since leathery soles, and well-brushed furry feet are a feature of essential hobbitness, he ought really to appear unbooted, except in special illustrations of episodes.'

A rough sketch by Tolkien (fig. 40) seems to illustrate the flight of the eagles in chapter 7, carrying the travellers from the eyrie in the Misty Mountains down to the lands near the Great River of Wilderland: 'The earth was much nearer, and below them were trees that looked like oaks and elms, and wide grass lands, and a river running through it all. But cropping out of the ground, right in the path of the stream which looped itself about it, was a great rock, almost a hill of stone. . . .' The 'great rock', called the 'Carrock' by Beorn, is at centre right in the picture. The final words of the inscription 'Eagles Eyrie, Eagles Flight, Gandalf at Door' refer to the drawing *Gandalf* (fig. 3), which is on the other side of the sheet.

Associated with these *Hobbit* illustrations by subject is an early water-colour by Tolkien, *The Misty Mountains* (fig. 35). Despite its title, it is probably another echo of the Alps rather than an illustration of the Misty Mountains named in *The Hobbit*. In this picture also is a motif often seen in Tolkien's art: a road (or path) leading into the distance, to some place known only in the imagination.

Beorn's Hall

All of Tolkien's pictures of the interior of Beorn's house depict a hall similar in design to ancient Norse or Germanic halls, constructed of timber and with a central fire-pit. Smoke from the fire rises through a hole or shutter which also admits light during the day. Thus in chapter 7 of *The Hobbit*, Bilbo and Gandalf follow Beorn and enter 'a wide hall with a fire-place in the middle. Though it was summer there was a wood-fire burning and the smoke was rising to the blackened rafters in search of the way out through an opening in the roof.' As in the veranda to which the visitors are shown later, the wooden posts of the hall are 'made of single tree-trunks', drawn with decorative branching at the top.

Firelight in Beorn's House (fig. 41) bears a strong, and probably not coincidental, resemblance to an illustration in *An Introduction to Old Norse* (1927) by Tolkien's friend and colleague E.V. Gordon (who, however, had the picture from even earlier sources). Here the posts stand on rounded bases, and there is only a low table or bench beside the fire. *Firelight in Beorn's House* comes to life with a small addition of red ink, for the flames and the light cast by the fire, in an otherwise claustrophobic picture with heavy black lines and solids.

For the published *Hobbit*, Tolkien produced a new illustration with a more careful line. He began to create the composition, similar to that of *Firelight in Beorn's House*, in an untitled sketch (fig. 42) using a series of perspective lines. In another drawing (fig. 43), on the opposite side of the same sheet, the point of view is shifted to the left, and there are no horizontal braces as in the earlier picture. Here Tolkien also seems to have begun to draw one or two figures behind the second post on the left.

In the final drawing, *Beorn's Hall* (fig. 44), the room is taller and more spacious. One can now see the smoke-hole in the roof and the door at the far end of the hall, and the fire-pit is more contained, no longer running the length of the room. Next to the table are the 'round drum-shaped sections of logs, smoothed and polished, and low enough even for Bilbo' rolled in by Beorn's ponies. The glow of the fire is shown by an absence of ink lines on the central posts and floor.

Fire light in Beorn' s hou se

41. *Firelight in Beorn's House*

MS.T.ar.16

42. Sketch for *Beorn's Hall*

43. Sketch for *Beorn's Hall*

44. *Beorn's Hall*

Mirkwood

In the manuscript of *The Hobbit*, Tolkien paused in his writing to sketch a map of the Misty Mountains and the upper part of the Great River of Wilderland (known in *The Lord of the Rings* as the Anduin). Here Medved (as Beorn was known at this stage of invention) is advising the travellers as to their path once they leave his care: 'The goblins will not dare to cross the river at the Carrock or to come near my house – it is well protected at night! – but the river bends towards the forest northwards, and so do the mountains. . . .' The companions ride 'out a little gate from [Medved's] high hedges on the east side' and (beyond this point in the manuscript) travel north-east to the beginning of the path through the forest.

The sketch map (fig. 45) records important landmarks. At left, west of the Misty Mountains, is marked the pass taken in chapter 4. East of the mountains are 'Goblin gate', 'wargs', and 'pine woods'. At right are the Carrock in the Great River, Medved's home, and Mirkwood. The dashed line from the Carrock to the edge of the forest presumably was meant to begin at 'Medved', where the travellers depart in the story; at any rate, the route here proceeds north-east as in the draft.

But Tolkien revised this section so that Bilbo, Gandalf, and the dwarves turn north as they leave Beorn's 'high hedges at the east of his fenced lands', and then bear 'to the north-west. By his advice they were no longer making for the main forest-road to the south of his land', but for 'a few days' ride due north of the Carrock . . . the gate of a little-known pathway through Mirkwood that led almost straight towards the Lonely Mountain' (ch. 7). Reflecting this change, Tolkien drew, in ink and coloured pencil, a new map (fig. 46) based on his sketch. A dotted line to the south indicates the 'old track' from the mountain pass, which crosses the ford and continues east to the Old Forest Road; while north-west of Beorn's house is the 'forest gate' opening on to an 'Elf-path'.

This seems to have been one of the five maps Tolkien originally intended to include in the published *Hobbit*, and was asked to redraw in black ink alone to suit the line-block process. In the end, he abandoned it. All of its details, however, are included in the *Wilderland* map printed in *The Hobbit* as the back endpaper.

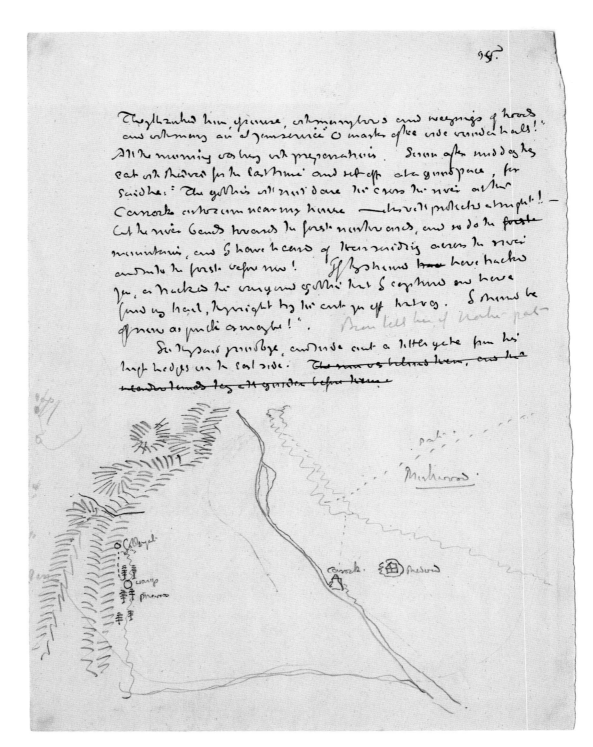

45. Page from the *Hobbit* manuscript with sketch map

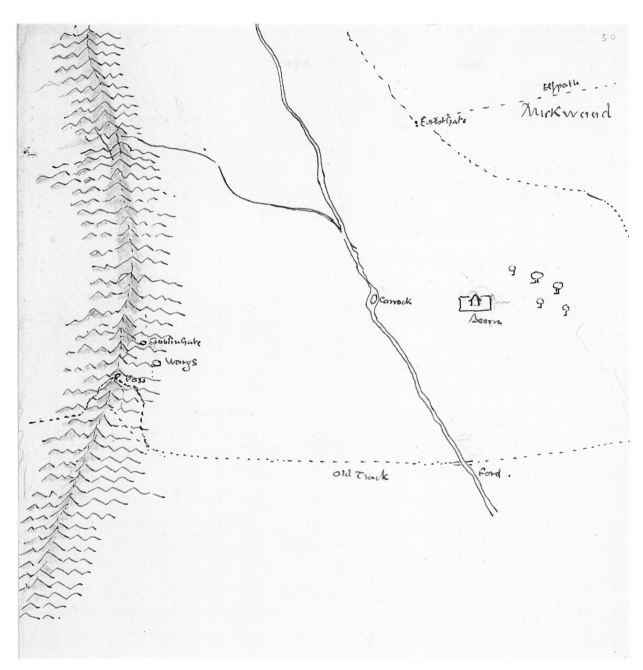

Elfpath

Eastgate

Mirkwood

Carrock

Beorn

Goblingate

Warys

Pass

Old Track

Ford.

46. Revised map of the Misty Mountains and the upper part of the Great River

When Tolkien first supplied illustrations for the published *Hobbit*, he hoped 'that they might serve as endpapers, frontispiece or what not'. In particular, though he did not say so at the time, he hoped that *Mirkwood* (fig. 47) would be printed on the front endpaper (instead of *Thror's Map*, which Allen & Unwin had suggested for that purpose). He had placed *Mirkwood* first among illustrations in the 'home manuscript', he said, without explaining why this had been so. At the least, it sets the scene for an adventure into dark and dangerous places in the Wild. It is also one of many expressions by Tolkien of ancient forests out of the cultural memory of Northern Europe: Nature at its most fearsome, mysterious and untamed. In chapter 8 of *The Hobbit*, Bilbo glimpses unfamiliar creatures and hears 'grunts, scufflings, and hurryings in the undergrowth' of Mirkwood. Soon he and his companions grow 'sick for a sight of the sun and of the sky', and long 'for the feel of wind on their faces. There was no movement of air down under the forest-roof, and it was everlastingly still and dark and stuffy.'

Tolkien based *Mirkwood* on a colour drawing he had made for 'The Silmarillion', *Taur-na-Fúin* (fig. 48), illustrating a moment in the tale of Túrin Turambar. In *The Book of Lost Tales*, he described Taurfuin (an earlier name, which means 'Forest of Night') as 'a dark and perilous region so thick with pines of giant growth that none but the goblins might find a track'. Since Mirkwood in *The Hobbit* is at least an analogue of the great 'Silmarillion' forest, Tolkien was able to use almost the same image for both, in the *Hobbit* version omitting the elves and adding mushrooms and a spider. Later, he added the title *Fangorn Forest* so that the picture might serve, in a pinch, also as an illustration for *The Lord of the Rings*.

Because Tolkien used ink washes to create the gloom of Mirkwood, Allen & Unwin had to print the drawing as an inserted half-tone (photographed as line art, the grey ink would have turned black or white). Happily, the publisher was willing to do so despite the added cost, though *Mirkwood* was omitted from the illustrations after the second printing. The picture also appeared in the first American edition of *The Hobbit*, but was redrawn in line, almost certainly by another artist. Since the original art has been lost – Tolkien gave it to a student – in the present book *Mirkwood* has been reproduced from the published plate.

47. *Mirkwood*

48. *Taur-na-Fúin* (*Fangorn Forest*)

The Elvenking's Gate

In chapter 9 of *The Hobbit*, the dwarves are captured by Wood-elves and brought to the halls of the Elvenking, over a bridge across the Forest River: 'The water flowed dark and swift and strong beneath; and at the far end were gates before the mouth of a huge cave that ran into the side of a steep slope covered with trees. There the great beeches came right down to the bank, till their feet were in the stream.' Tolkien's illustrations of the entrance to the Elvenking's halls are as numerous as those of Hobbiton and The Hill, but with greater variation. As with that other series, it is impossible to be sure of the order of creation, though educated guesses can be made based on differences in style and changes of detail.

The earliest 'Elvenking's gate' picture, perhaps even earlier than the relevant text, seems to be one drawn with a heavy application of ink (fig. 49). In the opening of the cave, beyond a prominent bridge, are rudimentary gates made of wood – hardly what one expects at the entrance to a king's palace, nor are they the 'huge doors of stone' described in chapter 8 (a phrase present even in the manuscript of *The Hobbit*), though they might conceivably close 'with a clang' (ch. 9).

For another untitled, but unfinished, view (fig. 50), Tolkien chose a more distant vantage point. A bridge spans a river painted blue, but the mouth of the cave has no visible doors. Unique among these pictures, the scene appears to be set under a moon in an overcast sky (in *The Hobbit*, the dwarves are brought to the king after dark, by torch-light). *Entrance to the Elvenking's Halls* (fig. 51) has a similar composition, but with large trees in the foreground. This seems to have been followed by an untitled picture (fig. 52) in which Tolkien again shifted the point of view, altered the landscape, and added a flight of steps from the bridge to the cave, where the opening appears to contain tall spikes.

In *Gate of the Elvenking's Halls* (fig. 53) the view is from a bird's eye, revealing more of the surrounding countryside. The mouth of the cave is now shaped like the Greek letter *pi* (π) and is covered by massive doors. Tolkien added shadows in pencil and ink wash, and he drew, then erased (though not completely), a blazing sun in the sky at upper right.

49. Entrance to the Elvenking's halls

The design of *Gate of the Elvenking's Halls* is very like that of two of Tolkien's pictures of the entrance to Nargothrond, an underground stronghold of elves in 'The Silmarillion' of which the halls of the Wood-elves in *The Hobbit* are a close analogue. In these illustrations too, the gateways are *pi*-shaped (trilithons), with posts and lintels. Tolkien made the painting (fig. 54) first, in the summer of 1928, but abandoned it without roughing in, except for a pencil line, the adjacent river Narog and the opposite shore. (At some point, spots of water fell on this sheet, causing colours to run.) The later ink drawing of the entrance (fig. 55) is clearly based on the water-colour, but with a more developed landscape and a slender arched bridge, not unlike the 'narrow bridge of stone' in most of Tolkien's images of Rivendell.

Christopher Tolkien has suggested that in his father's imagination the entrances to Nargothrond and the Elvenking's halls 'were visually one, or little distinguished: a single image with more than one emergence in the legends'. The similarities between these pictures, particularly the lines of the hills and the shape of the caves, are striking and surely deliberate: not only the ink drawing of Nargothrond, but also three illustrations for *The Hobbit* (figs. 73, 74, 75), are on the backs of leaves from the same discarded philological manuscript by Tolkien, and so may have been made at around the same time. But there are also differences, most notably that Nargothrond has three cave-like entrances while the Wood-elves' fortress has only one.

Another drawing of the entrance (fig. 56) is similar to one of the pictures 'framed' with trees (fig. 52), and may have followed on from that, or it may have been an attempt to revise *Gate of the Elvenking's Halls* in a simpler manner. In the end, Tolkien returned to the point of view with which he began, directly in front of the doors, while incorporating elements of his various trials. *Elfking's Gate* (fig. 57, on the other side of the sheet containing fig. 56) looks down an avenue of tall trees to the bridge, stairs, and cave. For the final, published illustration, *The Elvenking's Gate* (fig. 58), Tolkien extended the composition horizontally, adding to the frame of trees, and for added depth, used a gentle S-curve to carry the eye beyond the entrance, up and to the top of a distant hill.

54. *Nargothrond*

55. Nargothrond

56. Entrance to the Elvenking's halls

57. *Elfking's Gate*

The Elvenking's Gate.

58. *The Elvenking's Gate*

59. Entrances to the Elvenking's halls

The Forest River

The water-colour *Sketch for The Forest River* (fig. 61), preceded by a faint pencil drawing (fig. 60), was Tolkien's first attempt to illustrate the arrival of Bilbo at the eastern edge of Mirkwood after he and the dwarves escape from the halls of the Elvenking. Bilbo is shown (still in boots) riding one of the barrels from the king's wine cellars. As in *The Hobbit*, he has come to the raft-elves' bay during the night-time: 'In this way at last Mr. Baggins came to a place where the trees on either hand grew thinner. . . . The dark river opened suddenly wide, and there it was joined to the main water of the Forest River flowing down in haste from the king's great doors. There was a dim sheet of water no longer overshadowed, and on its sliding surface there were dancing and broken reflections of clouds and of stars' (ch. 9). At upper right are the huts of the raft-elves, lights in their windows, near the 'little jutting cape of hard rock' and 'shingly shore under hanging banks'.

There is only one barrel to be seen, however, out of the 'company of casks and tubs' said to run aground or 'bump against the stony pier'. More seriously, Bilbo seems to be on the main, or southern, branch of the Forest River, rather than the northern part suggested by the text and the *Wilderland* map. Tolkien evidently realized that he had made an error of geography, for in the presumably later drawing *The Forest River* (fig. 62) the stream curves to the right, which is correct for the northern branch joining the 'main water'.

The published illustration, *Bilbo Comes to the Huts of the Raft-elves* (fig. 64), another of the colour pictures Tolkien made for his American publisher, Houghton Mifflin (but which was omitted from their edition of *The Hobbit*), is said to have been his favourite among his paintings. The southern branch of the river is seen entering from the right, and there are now five barrels in the stream besides those that have already reached the shore and the one the hobbit is riding. That Bilbo is shown to arrive in daylight rather than after dark, and with no suggestion that he is invisible at this point in the story, are matters of artistic licence. Tolkien developed this painting through at least two sketches, one of which (fig. 63) is a more open composition with a single tall tree. (See also fig. 105.)

Bilbo comes to the Huts of the Raft-elves

64. *Bilbo Comes to the Huts of the Raft-elves*

Lake-town

Esgaroth, 'not far from the mouth of the Forest River', was 'not built on the shore, though there were a few huts and buildings there, but right out on the surface of the lake. . . . A great bridge made of wood ran out to where on huge piles made of forest trees was built a busy wooden town . . .' (ch. 10). Here the raft of barrels guided down river by the elves is 'moored not far from the shoreward head' of the bridge. In both of Tolkien's ink drawings of this settlement, the town proper is drawn meticulously, with many shapes and textures. *Esgaroth* (fig. 65), however, in other respects is only a sketch. At left, among the barrels, is the start of an abandoned ink wash. And although it is interesting to see the two bearded figures emerging from barrels on the shore, in the story Bilbo frees the dwarves out of the sight of men, after 'the shades of night' have fallen.

For publication in *The Hobbit*, Tolkien redrew *Esgaroth* as a more general view of life on the Long Lake. In *Lake Town* (fig. 66) there are more buildings, and heavier lines and shadows make them seem more substantial. Two swan-headed boats are on the lake rather than one, and the raft at bottom centre, on rippling water representing the end of the Forest River, is now tended by a pole-man. At centre right, a water-gate for craft to pass underneath the buildings has been added near one of the 'many steps and ladders going down to the surface of the lake'. At centre left, the guardhouse, which in *Esgaroth* is attached to the head of the bridge, has been moved further onto the shore, behind a stylized tree. Wisps of cloud now add interest to the sky. The pencil shading visible in the present reproduction, particularly on the shore at left, dropped out when printed in *The Hobbit* because it was too light to register in the blockmaker's camera.

It is generally accepted that Tolkien based the design of Lake-town on those of European prehistoric lake villages, and that he referred to images of them in a book when making his drawings. One possible source, reproduced in *J.R.R. Tolkien: Artist and Illustrator* (fig. 125), is from *Les Stations lacustres d'Europe aux âges de la pierre et du bronze* (1908) by Robert Munro. Others are given in the revised edition of Douglas A. Anderson's *Annotated Hobbit*.

ESGAROTH.

65. *Esgaroth*

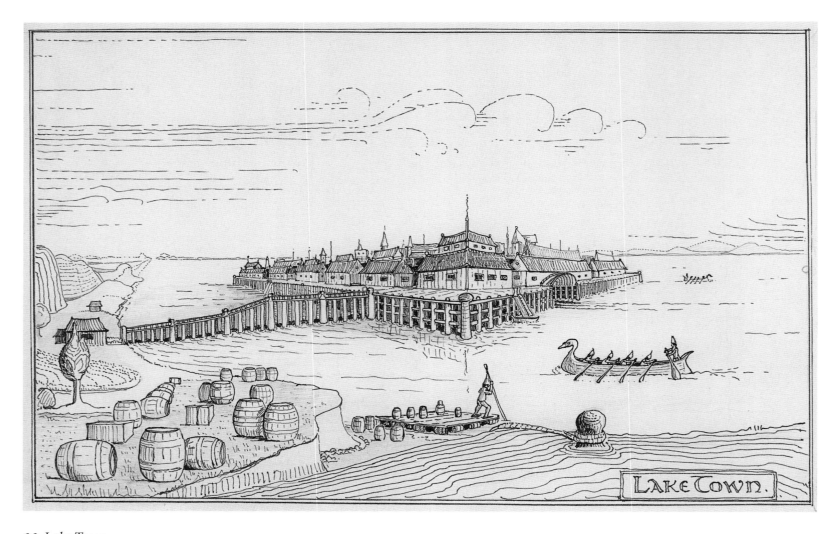

66. *Lake Town*

The Front Gate

Beyond the end of the southern spur of the Lonely Mountain, Bilbo and the dwarves see a 'dark cavernous opening in a great cliff-wall' between the mountain's arms. 'Out of it the waters of the Running River sprang; and out of it too there came a steam and a dark smoke' (ch. 11). *The Front Gate* (fig. 68) illustrates this steaming archway and the beginning of the river as it rushes, 'foaming and splashing among many boulders', towards the valley of Dale. The ground is 'bare and rocky', with only stray skeletons of trees to suggest that it once had life, before the dragon laid waste to the surrounding lands. Here a gnarled tree recalls not only those drawn in miniature around the Lonely Mountain in both of the published *Hobbit* maps, but also a sketch Tolkien made in 1928 (fig. 67), probably related to Grendel's mere from the Old English poem *Beowulf*.

As in some of his other drawings of mountains, such as *Rivendell Looking West* and *Rivendell Looking East* (figs. 20, 21), Tolkien used a variety of contour lines in *The Front Gate* to indicate banks, outcrops, slopes, and shadows. In the original drawing reproduced here in half-tone, one can see that Tolkien applied a dark grey wash to the river, to the lower part of the mountain above the arch of the gate, and to a wedge of rocks on the hill at left: these areas became solid black in the line-block process, and are printed as such in *The Hobbit*.

Tolkien also sketched the secret gate on the west side of the Lonely Mountain, with eight figures peering over a cliff-edge, walking on the heights, sitting or working. *The Back Door* (fig. 69) alludes to several scenes in chapter 11: 'Looking down [Bilbo and the dwarves] saw that they were at the top of the cliff at the valley's head and were gazing down on to their own camp below. Silently, clinging to the rocky wall on their right, they went in single file along the ledge, till the wall opened and they turned into a little steep-walled bay, grassy-floored, still and quiet.' Some of the dwarves are exploring 'a path that led higher and higher on to the mountain'. One is using a pick or mattock brought from Lake-town, while another is lowering a rope to the camp below. The 'door five feet high and three broad' is open, revealing a shaft leading down into the mountain and a dwarf at its threshold.

The shape of the secret entrance, like that of the Elvenking's gate, is a trapezoid. Three sides of it are sketched with long strokes in the picture *View from Back Door* (fig. 70). Beyond this 'window' are the rock-wall seen from the other direction in *The Back Door*, the Desolation of Smaug around the mountain with its withered trees, and the sun on the far horizon. This is the view seen by Bilbo near the end of chapter 11, when he does 'nothing but sit with his back to the rock-face and stare away west through the opening, over the cliff, over the wide lands to the black wall of Mirkwood, and to the distances beyond, in which he sometimes thought he could catch glimpses of the Misty Mountains small and far. . . . Soon he saw the orange ball of the sun sinking towards the level of his eyes.'

Tolkien also used this page to draw a revision to one of his discarded maps for *The Hobbit* (compare fig. 83). A rudimentary sketch of the Lonely Mountain is at left, its shape recalling the star-shaped rendering in *Thror's Map*, with the River Running flowing around Dale, its direction altered by Tolkien only after the text was in proof. The marshes east of the Elvenking's halls are drawn lightly at bottom.

67. Gnarled tree

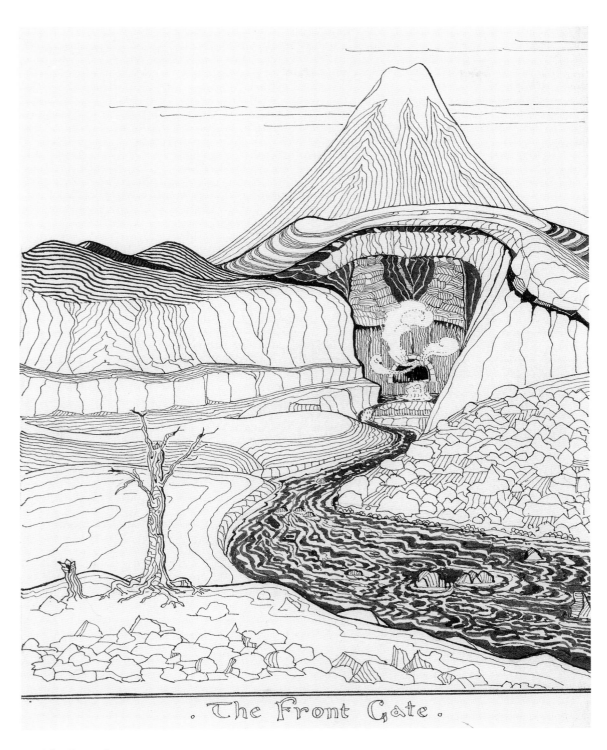

. The Front Gate .

68. *The Front Gate*

69. *The Back Door*

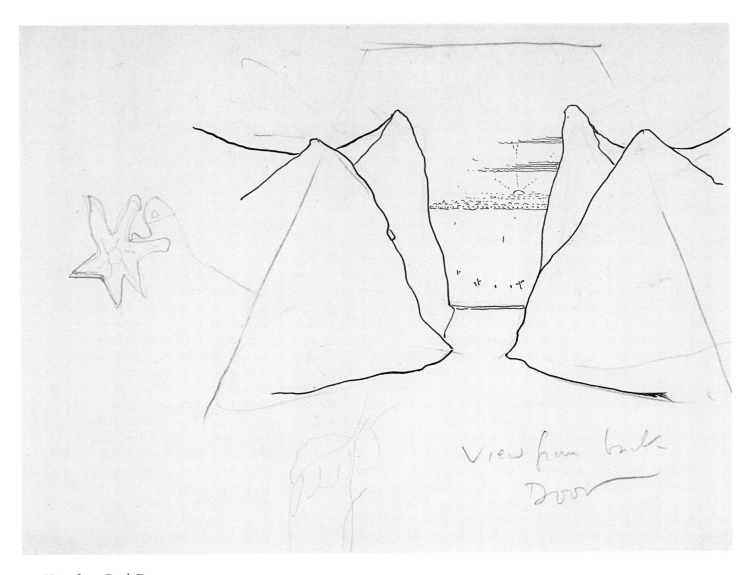

70. *View from Back Door*

71. *Conversation with Smaug*

104

Conversation with Smaug

Bilbo twice enters the lair of the dragon Smaug inside the Lonely Mountain. On his second visit, he is detected, and he and the great creature have a conversation. In the painting *Conversation with Smaug* (fig. 71), Tolkien illustrates the beginning of this episode, as the hobbit bows politely and addresses 'Smaug the Tremendous' and 'Smaug the Chiefest and Greatest of Calamities' (ch. 12). The cloud of vapour around the silhouette of Bilbo is meant to indicate that he cannot be seen while wearing Gollum's ring. Tolkien commented about this figure that, 'apart from being fat in the wrong places', it is 'enormously too large' relative to the dragon; 'but (as my children, at any rate, understand) he is really in a separate picture or "plane"'.

Smaug is 'a vast red-golden dragon', with emerald green on his head, hands, and body. Wisps of smoke rise from his nostrils. As he is first seen by Bilbo, 'under all his limbs and his huge coiled tail, and about him on all sides stretching away across the unseen floors, lay countless piles of precious things, gold wrought and unwrought, gems and jewels, and silver red-stained in the ruddy light. . . . Behind him where the walls were nearest could dimly be seen coats of mail, helms and axes, swords and spears hanging; and there in rows stood great jars and vessels filled with a wealth that could not be guessed.' Of the dwarves that once lived in this great hall, only bones and discarded weapons remain. Circling bats and black fumes suggest that this is a very unhealthy place for a hobbit.

Shining like a star at the top of the vast hoard is presumably the Arkenstone, 'the great white gem, which the dwarves had found beneath the roots of the Mountain', to Thorin Oakenshield the most precious of treasures. To the left of the end of the dragon's tail may be 'the necklace of Girion, Lord of Dale, made of five hundred emeralds green as grass'. At lower left, the huge pot of gold and jewels – so tall that a ladder is needed to reach the top – is inscribed with a warning in *tengwar*. Part of it reads: *gold [of] Thror [and] Thrain accursed be the thief.* Other pots bear the TH-rune, for 'Thror' or 'Thrain', kings of the Dwarves under the Mountain.

Smaug Flies around the Mountain

When producing his *Hobbit* art, Tolkien borrowed twice from *The White Dragon Pursues Roverandom & the Moondog* (fig. 72), an illustration for his children's story *Roverandom*: the dragon appears again in *Wilderland* (fig. 89), and the large spider in *Mirkwood* (fig. 47). Another dragon, sketched above marching dwarves (fig. 73), was reused (more or less) in *Thror's Map* (fig. 28) and in the final art for the *Hobbit* dust-jacket (fig. 101); and both this image and the White Dragon are of a kind with the figure in four illustrations of Smaug flying around the Lonely Mountain. Smaug does so twice in chapter 12, after Bilbo steals a cup from the dragon's hoard, and after the conversation between dragon and hobbit.

Probably the earliest of these pictures, an untitled ink drawing with an elaborate sky (fig. 74), appears to be set in daylight, though in the story Smaug flies only at night. The dragon is black against the mountainside, as is the front gate and Ravenhill on the south-west spur. At the bend of the river are the remains of the old bridge that Bilbo and the dwarves cross in chapter 13 ('most of its stones were now only boulders in the shallow noisy stream'). Beyond it are the 'ancient steps' by which they climb the 'high bank', and the road running around the spur to the path leading up to the look-out post. At right are the ruins of Dale.

Tolkien also made a version of this picture, *Smaug Flies round the Mountain* (fig. 75), using water-colour, with few differences of detail. Two other drawings, *The Front Door* (fig. 76) and *The Lonely Mountain* (fig. 77), have decorative titling, and the latter is demonstrably set at night, the dragon a stark white against a jet-black sky. The most notable change in these later views, however, is the course of the river, which now winds 'a wide loop over the valley of Dale' (ch. 11). (It may be seen faintly sketched in the earlier view, fig. 74.) Tolkien made this alteration also in his revised *Thror's Map* (figs. 26, 28) around the end of 1936, but a corresponding change in the text only when the book was in proof. Although *The Front Door* and *The Lonely Mountain* are more finished drawings, neither seems to have been offered to Allen & Unwin for publication – made too late, maybe, or because they contain varied greys or dense blacks not well suited to line-blocks.

72. *The White Dragon Pursues Roverandom & the Moondog*

73. Smaug in flight and dwarves marching

74. Smaug flies around the Lonely Mountain

Smaug Flies Round the Mountain.

75. *Smaug Flies Round the Mountain*

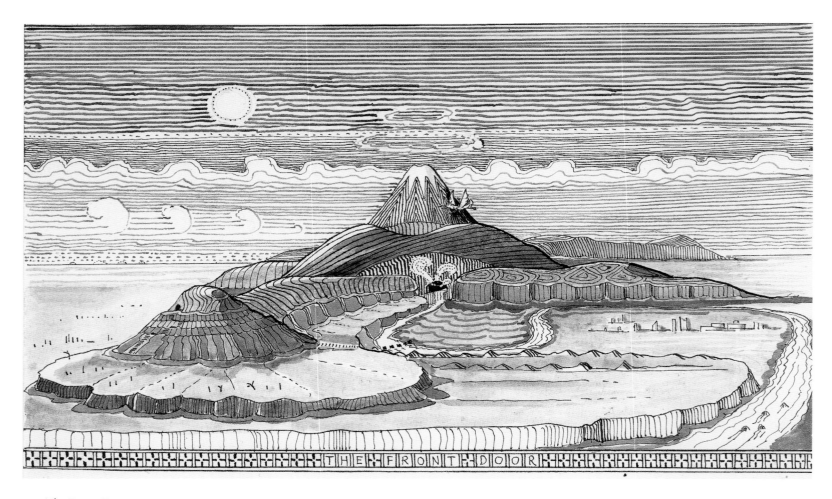

76. *The Front Door*

77. *The Lonely Mountain*

Death of Smaug

Tolkien illustrated the death of Smaug over Lake-town just at the fatal moment (fig. 78). Flames spring high from the burning buildings. The air is thick with smoke. The great bridge has been cast down into the water. The moon is up, and Bard the Bowman has shot his black arrow. In the distance, the summit of the Lonely Mountain is red and smoking like a volcano – though, as told in *The Hobbit*, the light from Smaug's fiery rage at the end of chapter 12 had faded well before he reached the Long Lake on his flight of vengeance.

Tolkien guessed, much later, that he made *Death of Smaug* around 1936. It seems possible, though, that it was instead an earlier aid to the writing of chapter 14; or perhaps it was a preliminary sketch for one of the colour pictures Tolkien agreed to produce in 1937, but in this instance he abandoned the subject. At any rate, it was not suitable for publication as it stood. Tolkien noted errors in its margins: 'The moon should be a *crescent*: it was only a few nights after the New Moon on Durin's Day' (thus a crescent shape is sketched within the moon's circle); 'Dragon should have a white *naked* spot where the arrow enters'; 'Bard the Bowman sh[oul]d be standing after release of arrow at extreme left point of the piles'. When Tolkien provided *Death of Smaug* to Allen & Unwin for their 1966 edition of *The Hobbit*, he was 'not very happy about the use of this scrawl as a cover. It seems too much in the modern mode in which those who can draw try to conceal it.' He hoped, rather, that it might help or inspire another artist to create a similar scene, and it may have been for this purpose that he used ink to strengthen the two marginal notes originally in pencil (at left) and to add a third (at bottom).

On the reverse side of this sheet (fig. 79), Tolkien used a convenient blank space to practice his calligraphy, English and *tengwar* (the two words at the top read *Ezgaroth* and *Esgaroth*; below 'The Death of Smaug' is *above Esgaroth upon the Long Lake*; and at the bottom is *Smaug the magnificent king of the dragons of the North*). But he also used this page for testing ink and water-colours, and if it is no coincidence that the colours here are some of those used in *Conversation with Smaug* (fig. 71), then *Death of Smaug* may have been the model for its dragon.

78. *Death of Smaug*

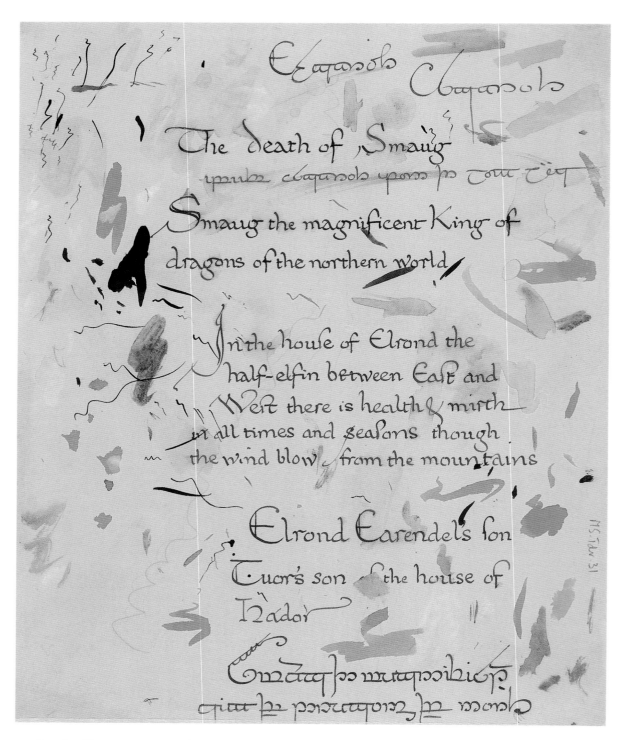

The death of Smaug

Smaug the magnificent King of
dragons of the northern world

In the house of Elrond the
half-elfin between East and
West there is health & mirth
in all times and seasons though
the wind blows from the mountains

Elrond Earendel's son
Tuor's son of the house of
Hador

79. *Death of Smaug,* reverse side of sheet

The Lonely Mountain and the Long Lake

With battle raging around the Lonely Mountain, Bilbo is on Ravenhill, wearing a helm and a coat of mail. 'The clouds were torn by the wind, and a red sunset slashed the West. [Bilbo] had seen a sight that made his heart leap, dark shapes small yet majestic against the distant glow. . . . "The Eagles! The Eagles!" Bilbo cried, dancing and waving his arms' (ch. 17). This is the subject of *The Coming of the Eagles* (fig. 80), though it is not clear which (if either) of the two figures is meant to be the hobbit. The title of the drawing is written at the top in *tengwar*.

As explained earlier, Tolkien originally intended to include in *The Hobbit* three regional maps in addition to *Thror's Map* and *Wilderland*. One of these seems to have been a map of the Lonely Mountain and surrounding lands. On a rough pencil sketch (fig. 81) are marked the Withered Heath, the Lonely Mountain, Mirkwood, marshland, the Forest River, and Lake-town. In another sketch (fig. 82), there are few labels: the words 'Withered Heath' are deleted, and 'Elfking' (the Elvenking's halls) is added above 'Mirkwood'. In a more detailed sketch (fig. 83), Tolkien elaborated the marshes near the end of the Forest River, the hills to the north-east, and features of the Long Lake. Later, he added sketches of the star-shaped mountain and the River Running while changing its course to loop around Dale.

Tolkien also drew two diagrams of the Lonely Mountain (figs. 84, 85), with important features labelled. New to these is the indication 'Approach to the Perilous Path', that is, to the secret door. *View through B[ack] G[ate]* (fig. 86) combines a sketch of the south-west spur of the Lonely Mountain and one of the Back Door seen between large rocks, both preliminary to details in the diagrams.

Finally, Tolkien made a coloured drawing of the Lonely Mountain (fig. 87), also with some of its features marked, notably 'Secret Door above the green western valley'. This is early enough that the river does not yet flow around Dale. On the same page is a small map of the Long Lake, showing the entrance of the River Running, Esgaroth with its great bridge, falls at the southern end of the lake, and the approach to the lake from the Forest River through marshes to the west.

80. *The Coming of the Eagles*

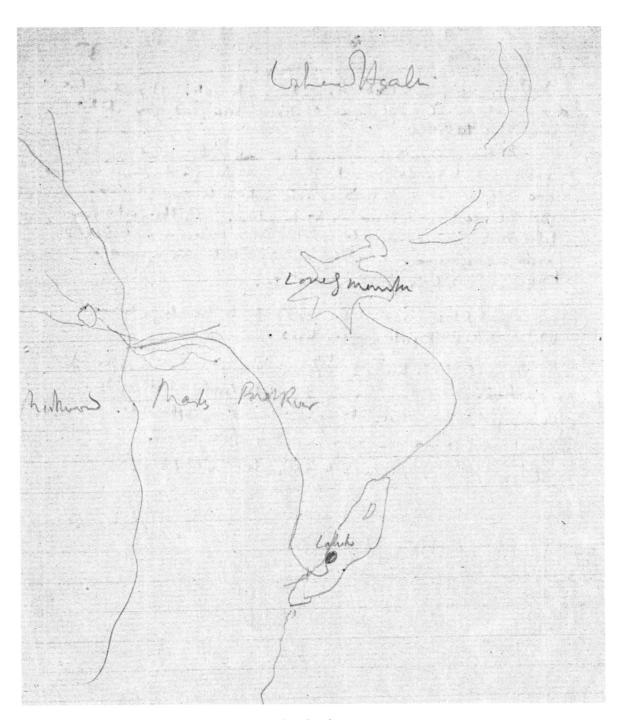

81. Map of the Lonely Mountain and surrounding lands

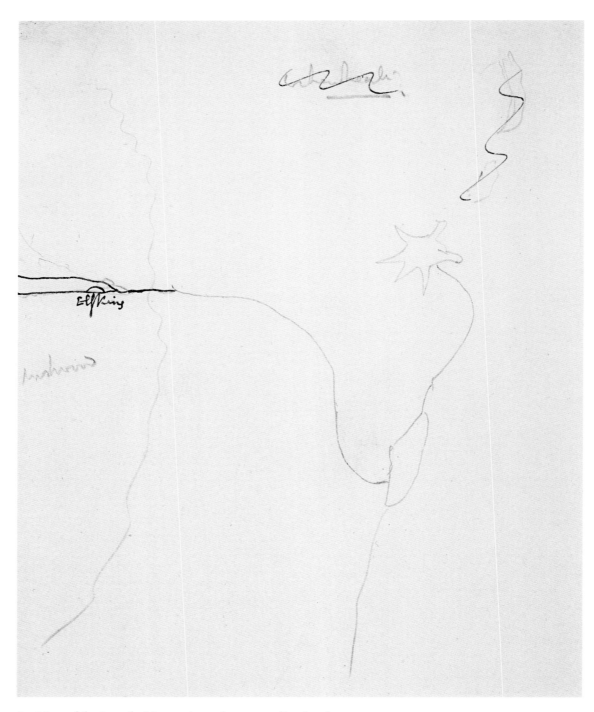

82. Map of the Lonely Mountain and surrounding lands

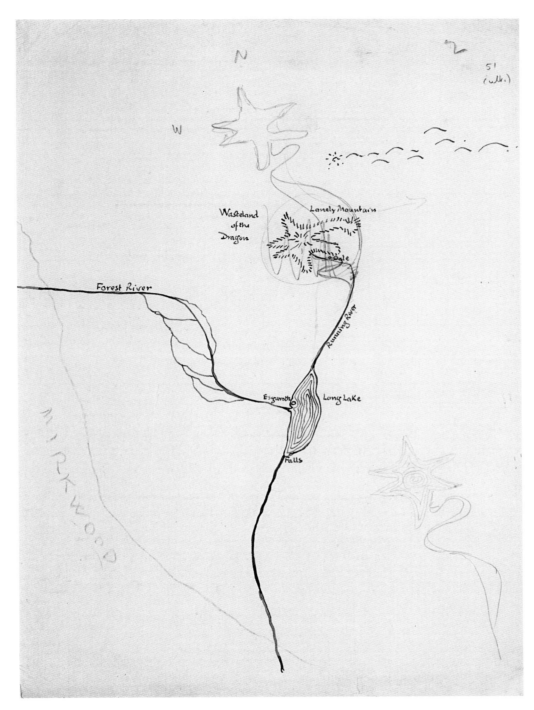

83. Map of the Lonely Mountain and surrounding lands

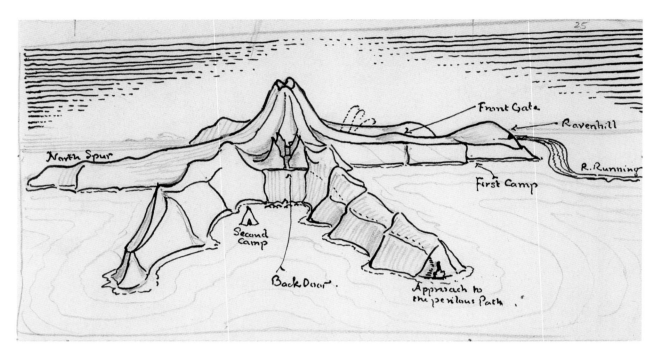

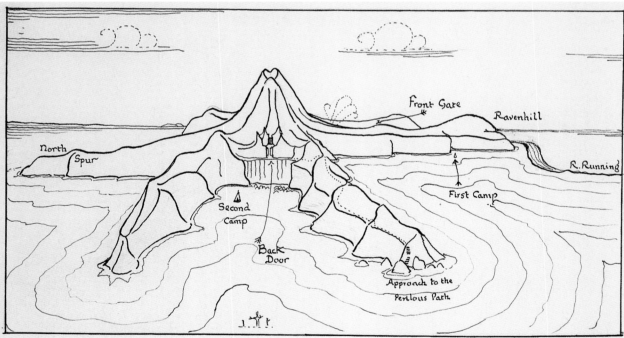

84, 85. Plans of the Lonely Mountain

86. *View through B[ack] G[ate]*

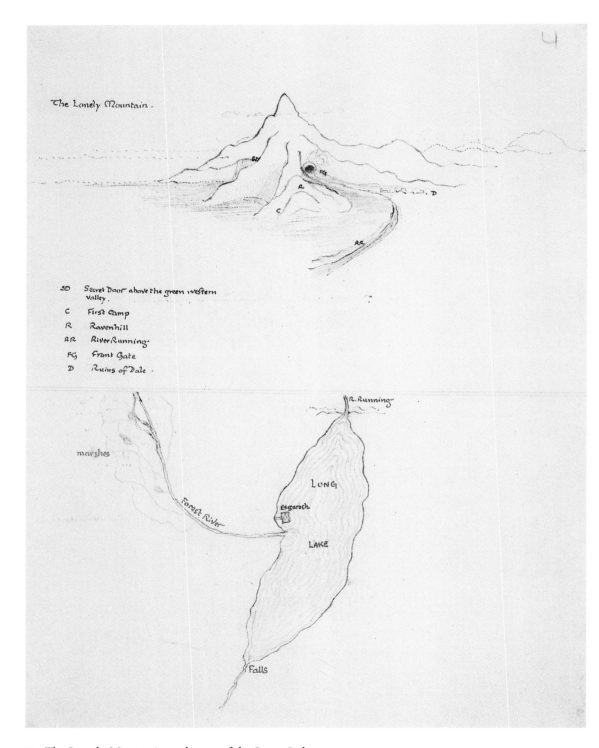

The Lonely Mountain.

SD Secret Door above the green western valley.
C   First Camp
R   Ravenhill
RR River Running.
FG Front Gate
D   Ruins of Dale.

R. Running

marshes

Forest River

Esgaroth

LONG

LAKE

Falls

87. *The Lonely Mountain* and map of the Long Lake

Wilderland

Here we return to the opinion of Rayner Unwin quoted at the start of our introduction: that *The Hobbit* needs maps as an aid to the reader. A story of a long journey, like *The Hobbit*, makes more sense to its reader if there is a map to show the route – or at least some of the route, if not in this instance entirely 'there and back again' from Hobbiton. *Wilderland* serves that purpose, but also provides, as Tolkien said of the *Lord of the Rings* maps, 'more than a mere index to what is said in the text'. *Wilderland* is a model picturesque map. A version of it, probably the drawing reproduced overleaf (fig. 88), was at the end of the 'home manuscript'. This is a beautiful work, drawn in coloured pencil and two colours of ink, with delicate shading especially along the line of the Misty Mountains – and that was the trouble as far as Allen & Unwin were concerned. The map could not be reproduced in that form by line-block, and it was restricted by cost to only two colours. Tolkien was advised to show the mountains 'only by hatching in one colour, the higher ranges being indicated by closer hatching. The rivers may then be shown by parallel lines. Possibly it will be best to indicate Mirkwood in the same colour as the Mountains, leaving the second colour for all the paths and all the lettering. All that is needed with the lettering is that you should do it a little more neatly.'

Tolkien redrew the map as he was asked (fig. 89), but did much more to improve it than was suggested. His lettering now was not only neater than before, but also bolder and more decorative: the overall title is enclosed within an elaborate frame. The mountains are distinguished not by two modes of hatching, but by hatching and solid blacks, giving a greater impression of depth. The contour lines that had described Mirkwood became a forest indeed, with individually drawn trees. The abbreviations of the first map are now spelled out, and in some cases renamed. There are also additions and changes, as small as the tiny tufts which indicate the marshes along the Forest River near the Long Lake, and as intriguing as the settlements of Woodmen in southern Mirkwood – they do not enter into a tale specifically until *The Lord of the Rings* – not to mention the ominous concentrations of spiders along the Elf-path in the north.

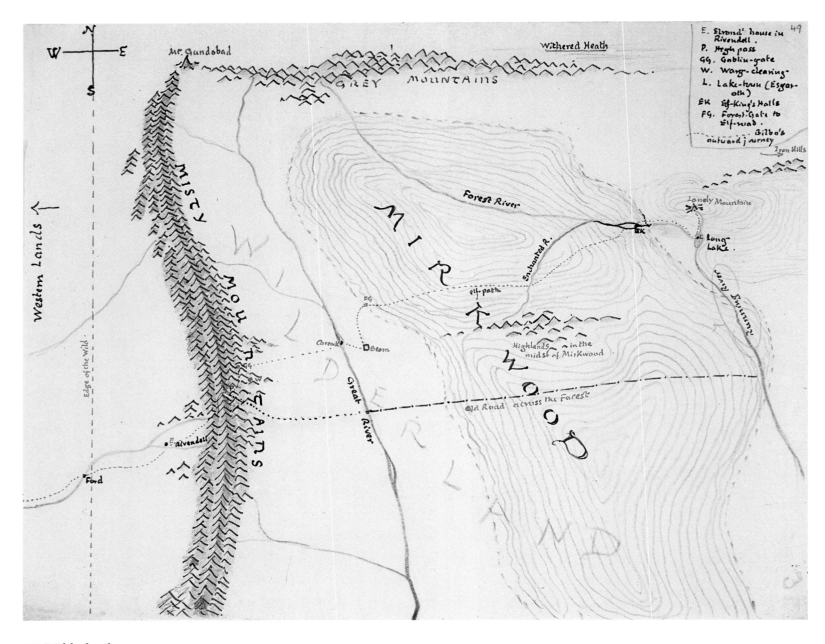

Legend (upper right):
- E. Elrond' house in Rivendell.
- P. High pass
- GG. Goblin-gate
- W. Warg-clearing
- L. Lake-town (Esgaroth)
- EK Elf-King's Halls
- FG. Forest-Gate to Elf-road.
- ······ Bilbo's outward journey

49

Map labels:
Withered Heath
Mt. Gundobad
GREY MOUNTAINS
W N E S
MISTY MOUNTAINS
Western Lands
Edge of the Wild
Ford
Rivendell
Carrock
Beorn
Great River
Old Road across the Forest
MIRKWOOD
WILDERLAND
Forest River
elf-path
Enchanted R.
FG
Highlands in the midst of Mirkwood
EK
Lonely Mountains
Long Lake
Running River
Iron Hills

88. Wilderland

124

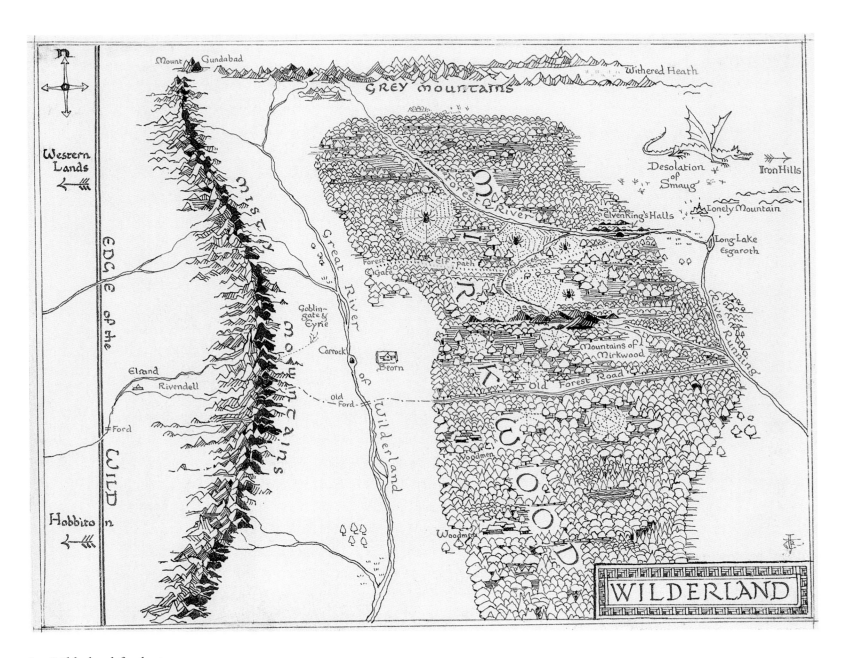

89. *Wilderland*, final art

The Hall at Bag-End

In *The Hall at Bag-End, Residence of B. Baggins Esquire* (fig. 90), the final illustration in *The Hobbit*, Bilbo returns to the pleasant existence in which the reader first met him. Now at last we see inside his home, if only part of it. But the entrance alone offers much of interest: 'The door opened on to a tube-shaped hall like a tunnel: a very comfortable tunnel without smoke, with panelled walls, and floors tiled and carpeted, provided with polished chairs, and lots and lots of pegs for hats and coats' (ch. 1).

In this residence, Tolkien says in *The Hobbit*, Bilbo 'remained very happy to the end of his days' (ch. 19). It is a fairy-tale ending to a story which contains among its dwarves, dragon, elves, and wizard many elements associated with fairy-tales. Bag-End in contrast is an oasis of familiarity. Chairs, tables, mirrors, rugs, a clock, a barometer, a lamp, a tobacco jar, a stand for umbrellas or walking-sticks are all recognizable in this picture. Its furnishings recall those of an English house of the early 20th century or the late 19th, and have given enthusiasts cause to speculate about Hobbit society, though Tolkien admitted that he did not design it down to its finer points. It was more important for him to establish, in *The Hobbit* as later in *The Lord of the Rings*, a place from which his hero could set out which the reader would recognize as a home to which a hobbit would wish to return.

The perspective is awkward: the chair on the left in particular is impossibly small. As drawn, the large door must have been difficult for someone of Bilbo's height to open or close, and the bell-pull seems uncomfortably high for a hobbit – or a company of dwarves. Behind the door is a shadow which Tolkien misguidedly applied with ink wash; in the line-block process, this became solid black and obscured a key in the lock.

Just as significant in the picture, however, is the view from the hall away from Bag-End. A lane begins at Bilbo's front step, between the potted shrubs, and continues down and around The Hill. We know from the pictures of Hobbiton where it goes from there. For Tolkien the storyteller, roads lead to adventure, 'ever ever on' towards the distant horizon, and the open door is our invitation to the journey.

The Hall at Bag-End, Residence of B. Baggins Esquire

90. *The Hall at Bag-End, Residence of B. Baggins Esquire*

91. Designs for the upper binding

Binding Designs

The sample binding for *The Hobbit* proposed by Allen & Unwin had wavy lines which wrapped around the volume at the top and bottom edges, and two more, shorter wavy lines below the title on the upper cover. Tolkien objected to these, suggesting that 'a small design would be an improvement' and offering to produce one. After a short delay due to illness, he sent a comprehensive new binding scheme to Allen & Unwin in which he aimed to transform the generic wavy lines into 'something significant' to his story, with 'an ornamental dragon-formula'.

On one sheet of trial drawings (fig. 91), he sketched five dragons in varying poses, each with a long, twisting tail. He also played with different treatments for the cover title, using standard roman capitals or medieval uncial-style letters to replace the italics his publisher had suggested. In another design (fig. 92), the titling once again is in roman capitals, but more formally centred. The dragon at bottom is similar to the one on the final binding (fig. 98), where it was given a more simplified form. The dragon at top, drawn over a sketch of mountains, apparently was meant as an alternate choice. Tolkien commented to Allen & Unwin that 'the wavy mountains could have appeared at bottom or top, according to the dragon selected'.

Having a decorative frieze of mountains on the binding became as important to Tolkien as a 'dragon-formula'. He made numerous trials (figs. 93–95, 106) before choosing a repeating pattern which incorporates a moon and sun and harmonizes with elements in his dust-jacket art (figs. 100, 101). On two sheets of designs (figs. 96, 97), Tolkien indicated that the frieze should repeat at the top, and that the dragon printed on the front cover should be printed also on the back cover, but in mirror-reverse. He also played with decorations based on D- and TH-runes, with a sun motif below the publisher's name, and with suns and moons and the D-rune in combination, presumably alluding to Durin's Day (thus D for 'Durin'), 'when the last moon of Autumn and the sun are in the sky together' (ch. 3). As elsewhere, the TH-runes undoubtedly stand for 'Thror' and 'Thrain'. The simplified rune-formula on the spine of the final binding follows suit.

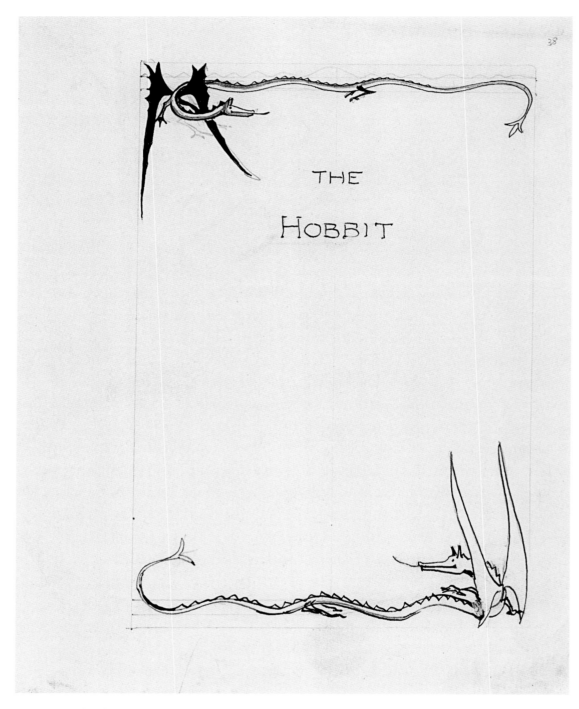

92. Design for the upper binding

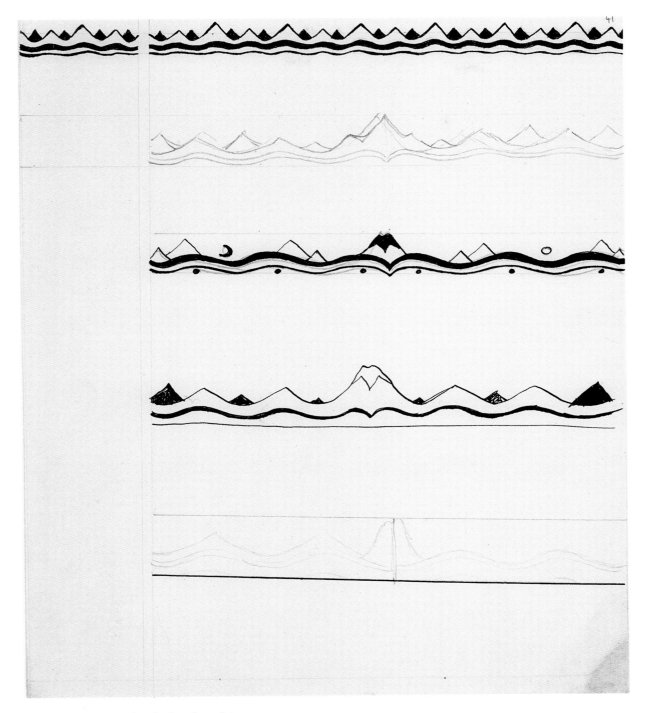

93. Trial drawings for the binding frieze

THE HOBBIT

THE HOBBIT

94, 95. Designs for the upper binding

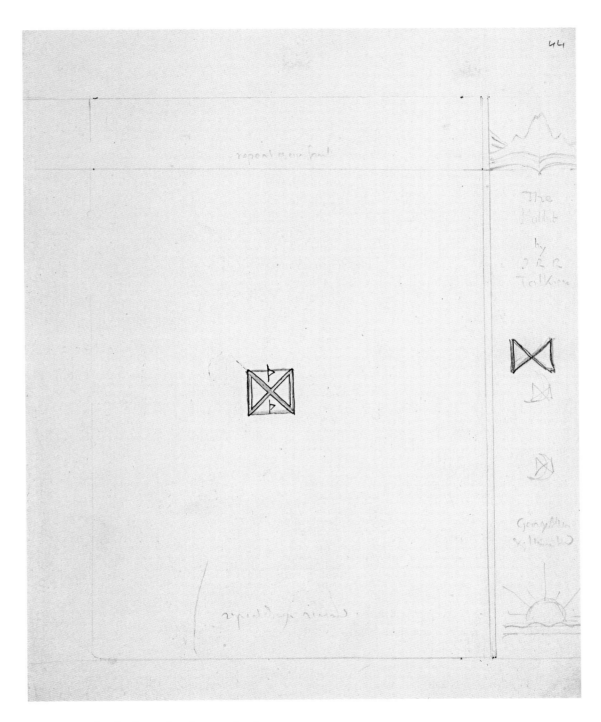

96. Design for the lower binding and spine

97. Designs for the lower binding and spine

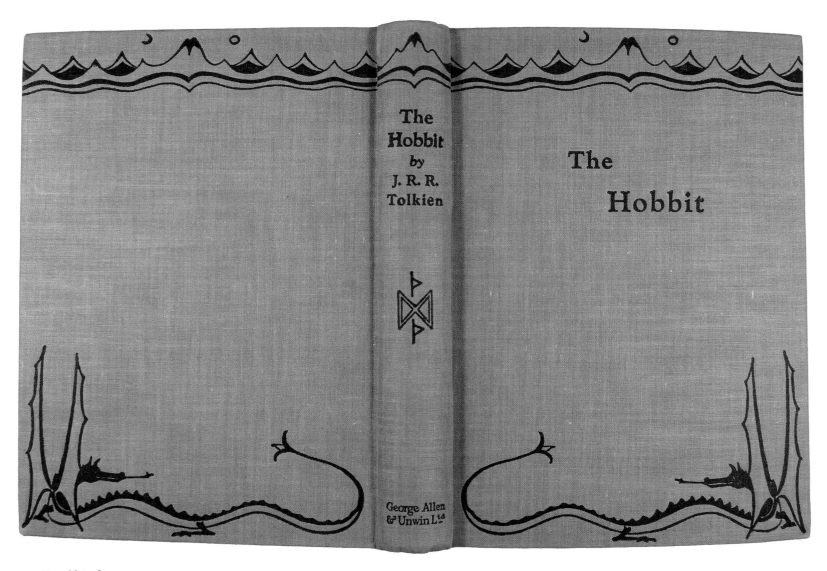

98. Final binding

Dust-jacket Art

Most of the trial dust-jackets Tolkien made for *The Hobbit* have been lost. The one that survives is only a fragment, preserved by mounting it on Japanese paper (fig. 100). It is probably one of the earliest of the jacket designs, as it seems never to have had the runic border present in the version Tolkien first sent to Allen & Unwin and which was used in the final art. Its foreground of woven trees and a sun shining above mountains or hills bears a strong resemblance to a painting by Tolkien from around 1928, *The Wood at the World's End* (fig. 99). The massed trees and central hill also recall his early illustration of the entrance to the Elvenking's halls (fig. 49).

Tolkien understood the cost of colour reproduction well enough to admit to Allen & Unwin that his first submitted sketch for the *Hobbit* dust-jacket had too many colours, including two reds and two greens in addition to blue and black. Production manager Charles Furth agreed, noting in particular the 'flush on the central mountain, which makes it look to our eyes just a trifle like a cake'.

99. *The Wood at the World's End*

100. Trial dust-jacket

101. Final dust-jacket art

Tolkien therefore reduced the number of colours to three – green, blue, and black – along with the white of the paper. Even so, he continued to feel that additional colours would be an advantage if effect alone were considered; and in case his publisher were to agree at the eleventh hour, he included notes of advice in the margins of the final dust-jacket art (fig. 101), in which the dragon and sun are coloured pink: 'omit red, & leave dragon white, if no red is used'; 'sun in thin outline (not cutting clouds) if no red used'; 'dark green (green patches behind last row of pointed trees) with wavy top edges on either side of path?'; 'front row of large trees dark green?'; 'if red is used author's name on shelf-back in red? Also (1) HOBBIT on front cover, & (2) blue under front row of *white* tree trunks (3) & outer runic border'. The heavy black bars at the top and bottom of the final art were provided by Tolkien as a means of adding height to the design in case, as he feared, he had drawn the jacket too wide. But he had not misjudged, and the bars were not needed.

The final dust-jacket was printed in three flat colours: green, blue, and black. Red has, however, been added to the covers of some later editions of *The Hobbit*.

In a letter to Allen & Unwin, Tolkien explained that 'the presence of the sun and moon in the sky together refers to the magic attaching to the door' in the Lonely Mountain – according to the hidden message on *Thror's Map*. The Lonely Mountain appears at the centre of the design, with a long road leading to it through deep woods and past, at right, the town of Esgaroth on the Long Lake. The border of Anglo-Saxon runes on the final dust-jacket reads: THE HOBBIT OR THERE AND BACK AGAIN BEING THE RECORD OF A YEARS JOURNEY MADE BY BILBO BAGGINS OF HOBBITON COMPILED FROM HIS MEMOIRS BY J.R.R. TOLKIEN AND PUBLISHED BY GEORGE ALLEN AND UNWIN LTD.

Although its lettering has since been revised by later hands, and the trim size of the book no longer fits the proportions of his design – on a taller, narrower volume, the left and right edges of the border now fold under with the flaps – Tolkien's dust-jacket for *The Hobbit* remains much as it was in 1937, still in use on some editions, and one of the most successful and inviting examples of British book cover art.

Portraits of Bilbo

Writing to his American publisher, Tolkien described a hobbit as 'a fairly human figure . . . fattish in the stomach, shortish in the leg. A round, jovial face; ears only slightly pointed and "elvish"; hair short and curling (brown). The feet from the ankles down, covered with brown hairy fur. Clothing: green velvet breeches; red or yellow waistcoat; brown or green jacket; gold (or brass) buttons; a dark green hood and cloak (belonging to a dwarf). . . . Actual size – only important if other objects are in [the] picture – say about three feet or three feet six inches.' He had been asked to draw hobbits in black and white for publicity purposes, and one in colour for a poster. Before replying, he made a quick, very rough sketch (fig. 102), possibly to confirm his view that the task should be left 'in the hands of someone who can draw. My own pictures are an unsafe guide – e.g. the picture of Mr. Baggins in Chapter VI [*Bilbo Woke Up with the Early Sun in His Eyes*] and XII [*Conversation with Smaug*]. The very ill-drawn one in Chapter XIX [*The Hall at Bag-End*] is a better guide than these in general impressions.' The reader may respond more charitably towards the portraits of Bilbo collected on the opposite page.

102. Sketch of a hobbit

103. Bilbo Baggins at home and abroad

Afterword

Of the many pictures Tolkien is known to have made for *The Hobbit,* only three are not featured on the preceding pages, chiefly for reasons of space. For the sake of completeness, we include them here at the end of the volume.

One (fig. 104) is a pencil sketch, no more than a few lines, of the 'V' of the cliffs through which the river flows in *Rivendell Looking West* (fig. 20), drawn on the other side of the same sheet. Another (fig. 105) is an intermediate sketch for *Bilbo Comes to the Huts of the Raft-elves* (fig. 64): here too the drawing is on the reverse of the sheet that also contains the finished picture, and is so faint that we have had to darken it heavily in order to bring out details for reproduction. Finally, there is a further drawing for the frieze of mountains on the *Hobbit* binding (fig. 106, on p. 144), almost but not quite the final version (which is shown on the binding itself in fig. 98).

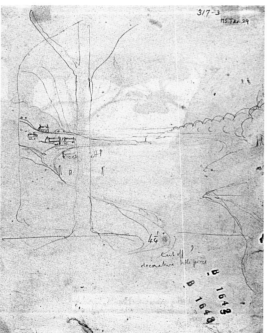

104

105

On the sketch for *Bilbo Comes to the Huts of the Raft-elves* there are (besides written and stamped reference numbers) two manuscript notes: '4¼″' and 'cut off? decorative title piece'. The first of these refers to the width of the picture as reproduced in the second British printing of *The Hobbit*, while the other asks if the decorative titling at the foot of the water-colour should be cropped. There seems to have been a question by production staff, on both sides of the Atlantic, whether to remove the titling integral to four of the five colour illustrations Tolkien made for *The Hobbit* in favour of printed captions. (Only *Bilbo Woke Up* has no decorative titling, but its title is present nonetheless, faintly written by Tolkien in the lower left corner, where it is largely overpainted.)

Tolkien had indicated, on sheets which accompanied his colour pictures, where in *The Hobbit* the plates should be inserted. For *The Hill: Hobbiton-across-the Water* he wrote: 'Frontispiece for "The Hobbit" (to be substituted, if required, for the similar black-and-white drawing)'. For each of the other plates, he cited a page number and a few words from the text with which the picture was to be associated. It seems unlikely that he meant these notes to become formal captions, but that is how they appear, in the list of illustrations and variously below the printed images, in the second Allen & Unwin and first Houghton Mifflin printings of *The Hobbit*, the first to include the colour plates. Allen & Unwin included the new frontispiece, the colour version of *The Hill*, as drawn, with the title-piece and Tolkien's monogram intact and no added caption; Houghton Mifflin cut off the titling and instead printed 'The Hill: Hobbiton across The Water' in type. In both editions, *Rivendell* is captioned 'The Fair Valley of Rivendell', but Allen & Unwin retained its decorative titling while Houghton Mifflin removed it. *Bilbo Woke Up with the Early Sun in His Eyes*, included only in the American edition, is titled thus as a printed caption. *Bilbo Comes to the Huts of the Raft-elves*, included only in the British edition and with its integral title retained, has the added words 'The dark river opened suddenly wide'. Finally, *Conversation with Smaug* has the printed caption '"O Smaug, the Chiefest and Greatest of [all] Calamities!"' – there is an extraneous 'all' in the British printing – but while Allen & Unwin preserved its decorative title-panel, Houghton Mifflin chose to paint it out.

The following images have been reproduced with the kind permission of the Bodleian Libraries, University of Oxford, from their holdings labelled *MS Tolkien Drawings*. In this list, Bodleian reference numbers are given in brackets, and indicate rectos unless specified as versos (= v): fig. 1 (1); fig. 2 (3); fig. 3 (2); fig. 4 (5); fig. 5 (4v); fig. 6 (4); fig. 7 (6v); fig. 8 (6); fig. 9 (89, fol. 12v); fig. 10 (7); fig. 11 (26); fig. 13 (8); fig. 14 (89, fol. 20); fig. 15 (89, fol. 21); fig. 16 (9); fig. 17 (89, fol. 17); fig. 18 (89, fol. 17v); fig. 19 (11v); fig. 20 (10); fig. 21 (12); fig. 22 (11); fig. 23 (27); fig. 25 (33); fig. 26 (22v); fig. 27 (87, fol. 39); fig. 28 (34); fig. 30 (33v); fig. 31 (89, fol. 37); fig. 32 (87, fol. 35); fig. 33 (34v); fig. 34 (13); fig. 35 (84, fol. 37); fig. 36 (88, fol. 21); fig. 37 (89, fol. 30); fig. 38 (14); fig. 39 (28); fig. 40 (2v); fig. 41 (15); fig. 42 (16v); fig. 43 (16); fig. 44 (17); fig. 46 (89, fol. 50); fig. 48 (89, fol. 14); fig. 49 (89, fol. 35): fig. 50 (89, fol. 36); fig. 51 (89, fol. 32); fig. 52 (89, fol. 31); fig. 53 (89, fol. 33); fig. 54 (87, fol. 46); fig. 55 (89, fol. 34); fig. 56 (18v); fig. 57 (18); fig. 58 (19); fig. 60 (89, fol. 47v); fig. 61 (21); fig. 62 (89, fol. 47); fig. 63 (20); fig. 64 (29); fig. 65 (22); fig. 66 (23); fig. 67 (88, fol. 20); fig. 68 (24); fig. 69 (89, fol. 48); fig. 70 (89, fol. 48v); fig. 71 (30); fig. 72 (89, fol. 3); fig. 73 (89, fol. 19); fig. 74 (89, fol. 22); fig. 75 (89, fol. 24); fig. 76 (89, fol. 23); fig. 77 (102); fig. 78 (31); fig. 79 (31v); fig. 80 (89, fol. 45); fig. 82 (89, fol. 50v); fig. 83 (89, fol. 51); fig. 84 (89, fol. 25); fig. 85 (89, fol. 46); fig. 86 (89, fol. 25v); fig. 87 (89, fol. 26); fig. 88 (89, fol. 49); fig. 89 (35); fig. 90 (25); fig. 91 (89, fol. 38v); fig. 92 (89, fol. 38); fig. 93 (89, fol. 41); fig. 94 (89, fol. 39); fig. 95 (89, fol. 40); fig. 96 (89, fol. 44); fig. 97 (89, fol. 43); fig. 99 (88, fol. 22); fig. 101 (32); fig. 104 (10v); fig. 105 (29v); fig. 106 (89, fol. 42).

The following images have been reproduced courtesy of the Department of Special Collections and University Archives, Raynor Memorial Libraries, Marquette University: fig. 24 (Additional Manuscripts 1, box 1, folder 1, fol. 1); fig. 29 (MS Tolkien series 1, box 2, folder 5, fol. 1); fig. 45 (MS Tolkien series 1, box 1, folder 7, fol. 10); fig. 81 (MS Tolkien series 1, box 1, folder 10, fol. 4v); fig. 100 (MS Tolkien series 1, box 2, folder 4).

Figs. 12 and 102 were supplied from HarperCollins files. Figs. 47 and 98, and the title spread on p. 6, were photographed from the authors' collection. The detail on the title-page is from fig. 34. The detail on the contents page is from fig. 101. Fig. 59 includes details from figs. 49, 50, 51, 52, 53, and 58. Fig. 103 includes details from figs. 1, 15, 39, 61, 64, 71, and 90.

Figs. 1–8, 10, 11, 13, 16, 19–26, 28–30, 33, 34, 38–45, 56–58, 61, 63–66, 68, 71, 77–79, 81, 89, 90, 98, 100, 101, 104, 105 are copyright © The J.R.R. Tolkien Copyright Trust 1937, 1938, 1966, 1976, 1978, 1987, 1989, 1992, 1995, 2011. Figs. 9, 12, 14, 15, 17, 18, 27, 31, 32, 35–37, 46–55, 60, 62, 67, 69, 70, 72–76, 80, 82–88, 91–97, 99, 102, 106 are copyright © The Tolkien Trust 1937, 1973, 1976, 1977, 1978, 1979, 1987, 1995, 2007, 2011. Quotations from *The Hobbit* are copyright © The J.R.R. Tolkien Copyright Trust 1937, 1951, 1966, 1978, 1995, 2002; from *The Fellowship of the Ring* (the first part of *The Lord of the Rings*) copyright © The J.R.R. Tolkien 1967 Discretionary Settlement and The Tolkien Trust 1954, 1966; from *The Book of Lost Tales, Part Two* copyright © The J.R.R. Tolkien Copyright Trust and C.R. Tolkien 1984; from letters and manuscripts by J.R.R. Tolkien copyright © The J.R.R. Tolkien Copyright Trust 1981, 1995, 2007, 2011. Quotations from letters in the Allen & Unwin archive are used with the permission of HarperCollins, successor to George Allen & Unwin and Unwin Hyman.

For supplying images for use in this book, we are grateful to Catherine Parker of the Bodleian Libraries, University of Oxford; Matt Blessing of the Department of Special Collections and University Archives of the Raynor Memorial Libraries, Marquette University; and Terence Caven of HarperCollins, London. Our thanks go also to David Brawn, publishing director for Tolkien projects at HarperCollins, for asking us to prepare this book, and to his associates Chris Smith and Natasha Hughes; to Cathleen Blackburn of Manches LLP, representing the Tolkien Estate; to Christopher Tolkien for assistance and permissions; and to Arden R. Smith for expert advice on languages and scripts.

106. Design for the binding frieze